Praise for
UNSHAKEN

Buried in the shattered depths of Haiti's devastating earthquake with no assurance of ever being rescued, Dan Woolley lived one of our worst nightmares. In this powerful story of the journey that his faith and courage took through that terrifying ordeal, you will be right there with him, moment by moment, unable to turn the pages fast enough to quiet your heart. Dan emerged from that dark and dusty tomb alive in so many ways — and *unshaken!* — with a vital message for all of us. Don't miss this!

WESS STAFFORD, president and CEO of Compassion International

———

The world followed Dan Woolley's story of courage and loss and eventual victory. Now we get the full, unvarnished truth about his struggle to live fully. This is a great story of God at work in the rubble of our lives. You won't leave its pages unchanged.

CHRIS FABRY, author and radio host

———

Dan Woolley takes his place in our Hall of Faith at Azusa Pacific University. We're honored to have him as a graduate because he is the finest example of living our university's "God First" motto. Dan survived an impossible human ordeal by keeping God first when the odds were completely against him. You will be inspired by the boldness of his honesty and faith.

JON R. WALLACE, DBA, president of Azusa Pacific University

UNSHAKEN

Rising from the Ruins
of Haiti's Hotel Montana

Dan Woolley
with Jennifer Schuchmann

ZONDERVAN®

ZONDERVAN.com/
AUTHORTRACKER
follow your favorite authors

ZONDERVAN

Unshaken
Copyright © 2011 by Daniel Woolley

This title is also available as a Zondervan ebook. Visit www.zondervan.com/ebooks.

This title is also available in a Zondervan audio edition. Visit www.zondervan.fm.

Requests for information should be addressed to:
Zondervan, *Grand Rapids, Michigan 49530*

Library of Congress Cataloging-in-Publication Data

Woolley, Dan.
    Unshaken : rising from the ruins of Haiti's Hotel Montana / Dan Woolley with Jennifer
  Schuchmann.
       p.   cm.
    ISBN 978-0-310-33097-4 (hardcover, jacketed)
    1. Consolation. 2. Woolley, Dan. 3. Haiti Earthquake, Haiti, 2010. 4. Earthquakes —
  Religious aspects — Christianity. 5. Suffering — Religious aspects — Christianity. 6. Trust in
  God — Christianity. I. Schuchmann, Jennifer, 1966- II. Title. III. Title: Rising from the ruins
  of Haiti's Hotel Montana.
  BV4909.W66 2010
  277.294'083092 — dc22
  [B]   2010034652

Cover design: *Curt Diepenhorst*
Cover photography: *Rick Loomis / Los Angeles Times*
Interior design: *Beth Shagene*

Printed in the United States of America

---

10 11 12 13 14 15 /DCI/ 24 23 22 21 20 19 18 17 16 15 14 13 12 11 10 9 8 7 6 5 4 3 2 1

To my wife, Christy,
from whom I learned the meaning of courage,
and in whom I found a reason to love.
I am yours — forever and always.
And to my sons, Joshua and Nathan.
You make me proud and give me hope for the future.

CONTENTS

PREFACE

Some may wonder why I have chosen to share this story of survival and rescue, especially since the stories of many others impacted by the earthquake did not end well, at least in human terms. I will never pretend to understand why God allowed me to be rescued, and though I celebrate with my family, I do not take lightly the difference between my outcome and the suffering of others. My story is truly a bittersweet one, and I live every day with the loss of those who did not survive that tragic day. I tell my story because I had an encounter with God in the midst of this crisis — my weakness meeting his strength — an encounter that has changed me forever, and one that I believe can bring hope to others. As a painter is drawn to set brush to canvas and a dancer starts to move when he hears music, I feel compelled to give voice to my experiences and testify to the grace of the God who was with me in the depths of my ruin.

It is for this purpose — to glorify God — that I was created, and this is the only reason for this book. I pray that as you face times of adversity, as well as times of abundance, you will also call out to our unshakable God.

Memory is a fickle friend, subject to time, aging brains, external influences, and even the limits of personal perception. Although I have made every attempt to accurately represent my experiences, I recognize my perception and memory were also affected by darkness, strong emotions, and a weakened physical condition. Where I was confused, I have tried to reconcile my understanding of events through the recollections of others who shared these situations. In some cases, I have allowed the confusion I felt to remain in the story so you can experience it with me (with subtle clues to alert you to it), just as I have tried to bring you along into my moments of fear or sadness. And though I did my best to recreate dialogue based on the essence of real conversations, there is no way I could document every word with complete accuracy.

I have made a few alterations to my story intentionally. For privacy reasons, I masked the identity of a few people, including some whom my wife, Christy, talked with, attributing those conversations in this account to different individuals. I also adjusted the spelling of Luckson's name (to Lukeson) to assist in pronunciation.

Many have asked me what I have learned through these experiences. The answer to that question keeps changing as more time passes. My answer on January 15 was different from what it was in April, which is different again from my answer in July 2010 when I was putting the finishing touches on this book. The lessons learned that I share in the final chapters represent a snapshot in time. Even now, my experiences still feel so new and raw that I expect the lessons I take away will continue to be refined over time. You can join me in this journey of discovery at www.Earthquake-Survivor.com.

Finally, more than at any time in my life, I have seen how fleeting is our time here on earth. If you find yourself moved by anything you read in this book, please take action. Right now. Don't let time, or the busyness of life, rob you of your resolve.

Invest yourself fully in those relationships you value most. Get your heart right with God and accept his grace. Perhaps join the fight against poverty and other injustice in the world. Whatever changes you feel called to make in your life, let this story be an effective catalyst to push you to action. Live this day, this moment, this breath, with full purpose and intentionality.

SOLI DEO GLORIA

I

BURIED IN HAITI

I spit out the blood and dust that coats my mouth, but I can't spit out the fear. Buried beneath six stories of rubble, the remains of what was once the Hotel Montana, I'm hanging on to the realization that I lived through an earthquake. I survived! But I also know that if I want to make it out of this black tomb alive, if I ever hope to see my family again, it will take a miracle — a series of miracles.

Miracles I'm not sure I have the faith to believe in.

In the complete darkness, I can't see a thing. The dust in my nose prevents me from smelling anything but concrete. I rub my arms and feel flecks of dust and debris sticking to the hairs. Wiping debris off my face, I can feel a paste where dust mixed with sweat. My body feels weak and broken. The fine powder collects on my eyelids, making them feel heavy. It would be easy to just close my eyes and drift off — to sleep, to death. But one thought keeps me awake and motivated: I have to live so I can get back to my family. How will my wife, Christy, react when she finds out I am buried in Haiti? It turns my stomach to think about her and the boys learning about the quake.

I need a place to rest and think about what to do next, but the elevator floor I'm sitting on is covered in jagged blocks of concrete and debris. I try to extend my legs, but the car is too small for my six-foot frame, and my feet touch the opposite wall. I try to adjust my body so that I am sitting diagonally to give myself room to stretch. I keep my legs spread apart so my knees don't touch and cause more pain in my leg wound. I had hoped that sitting still would diminish the pain, but with each beat of my heart my leg throbs with intense pain. I adjust my balled-up sock, putting it between my head and the wall to keep pressure on my wound. My thick hair feels sticky and warm to the touch — not a good sign. It means my head is still bleeding.

I'm getting tired, but I'm afraid to fall asleep. *What if I slip into unconsciousness?* Sleep feels like a significant threat — especially if I have a concussion or drift into shock. Even in the best case, sleep means giving up control of managing my circumstances. *I've survived an earthquake; I'm not going to die in my sleep.* I fumble for my iPhone and set the alarm to go off in twenty minutes. That way, even if I fall asleep, I won't nap long.

A poem by Dylan Thomas comes to mind. I had read it in college but hadn't thought of it in years. "Do not go gentle into that good night. Rage, rage against the dying of the light."

That's what I am going to do. I will rage against anything that might keep me from returning to my family. I take an inventory of my resources: my camera and iPhone, my passport, my journal, and a pen or two. Not much. I wonder if it is even possible to survive. And more importantly, if I don't, what might happen to my wife, Christy?

Christy had been diagnosed with clinical depression soon after we married. It took nearly six years before we were able to get it under control with therapy and medicine, but since then we'd enjoyed ten years of health and a happy marriage. Yet Christy and I both knew how quickly she could fall back into that black abyss. All it would take was a tragic event, something happening to one of our boys, or the death of one of her parents. With God's help, we had walked through her sickness together, but one thing we failed to anticipate was that something might happen to me.

Sitting in the darkness, I had to admit — things didn't look good.

I didn't sleep. I set my alarm again. And again. And yet again. That gave me the chance to assess my situation every twenty minutes. I wasn't sure I could hold on until rescuers arrived. Even in the worst disasters in the United States, buildings collapsed one or two at a time, not a whole city at a time. When people are trapped, professional rescuers — police, firefighters, and specially trained search and rescue teams — are on the scene in minutes, hours at most. They have trucks, equipment, extensive training, and experience. They have emergency plans, backup plans, and worst-case scenario plans.

But I wasn't in the United States.

I was buried in Haiti — one of the poorest countries in the world — and they had *nothing*. I was trapped in the wreckage of my collapsed hotel in an elevator car the size of a small shower. Despite all of that, I knew I was fortunate to be alive. I suspected that my colleague, David, had died instantly.

In order to survive, every decision I made had life-and-death consequences, but only one had eternal importance. *Could I trust God for whatever came next?* In the dark, with my head pressed against the elevator wall, I cried. Not for myself, but for Christy and the boys.

What would life be like for them if I died?

2

IN LIVING COLOR

Tuesday, January 12, 9:15 a.m. (EST)

Port-au-Prince, Haiti

"Good morning, Dan," Ephraim said as the SUV rolled to a stop in front of our hotel. "Are you ready to go to the church?"

"I'm ready and excited," I said as I helped David, the videographer for this trip, load our gear into the back of the car.

I had corresponded with Ephraim for several months planning this trip to Haiti, so I wasn't surprised when I found him waiting for us at the airport when we arrived on Monday. I immediately recognized his smile beaming out from underneath his straw hat with the bright tropical print on the band. After loading our luggage into his SUV, Ephraim took us to the Compassion International office in Port-au-Prince, where we spent the day with the local staff.

Though Ephraim and I were both employees of Compassion, we couldn't have been more different. He was physically one of the largest Haitian men I'd ever met. His stocky frame dwarfed my average build, and by comparison, his dark glistening skin made my olive complexion look pale. When I learned on Monday that Ephraim was assigned to be our guide for the rest of the week, I was pleased. Despite our physical differences, we had already connected around our common mission.

As I climbed in behind David, and settled in my seat, Ephraim's ebullient spirit seemed to overflow the SUV. I looked forward to the day's events — visiting a new Compassion program at a church just outside of the city and then making a home visit to one of the moms who participated in the program.

In the front seat next to Ephraim was Johnnie, a Haitian translator who helped Compassion and several other nonprofit organizations in Port-au-Prince. Johnnie was also tall and dark, slightly darker than Ephraim, but he was very thin.

While Ephraim didn't need a reason to laugh — he laughed at anything — Johnnie was more deliberate in his humor. He used his language skills to create a joke by carefully wordsmithing the conversation to evoke a laugh. Johnnie and Ephraim were like a vaudeville slapstick team — comedian and sidekick — keeping David and me entertained. I could tell they enjoyed working together.

———

As we drove up to the church and parked in the dirt lot next to it, I noticed the drab exterior of the one-story concrete building. I wondered what we'd find inside. We all exited the SUV eager to get started. Ephraim pushed his door shut, and the SUV rocked. Though his size may have been intimidating, his spirit wasn't. An inner joy danced across his face as he explained the program we would soon see inside the church.

"I'll introduce you to the pastor first," he said as he took off toward the front door. With his long strides, there was no point in trying to keep up with him. Ephraim had an undeniable sense of urgency about Compassion's work. Whenever he spoke about the difficulty of life in Haiti, he also talked about the difference Compassion was making for mothers and their children trapped in poverty. He understood the hardships of life in Haiti and chose to defy that reality by committing joyful acts of service for those who needed it most.

I guessed Ephraim was in his midfifties, but he had a boisterous life energy about him that belied a much younger man. His contagious smile filled his round face, and his hearty laugh made his whole body shake. He was like a monster-sized teddy bear just waiting for someone to hug.

I helped David grab the video camera and other equipment from the back of the SUV, and we hurried to catch up to Ephraim.

"Let's review what you want to accomplish today," David said as we walked.

"We need video that captures the Child Survival Program in action. I believe if people can *see* what Compassion is doing here, they'll want to support the ministry."

I'd only worked at Compassion International's headquarters in Colorado Springs for eighteen months, but I'd already learned a lot and I was impressed. Founded in 1952, Compassion is a Christian child development ministry that works to release children from spiritual, economic, social, and physical poverty. The long-term process can begin with prenatal care and continue through leadership training for qualified young adults who have earned an opportunity to attend a university. Compassion currently serves more than one million children in twenty-five countries worldwide. Though Compassion is perhaps best known for their child sponsorship programs — where donors form one-on-one relationships with their sponsored children through exchanging letters — in the past few years, new programs like the Child Survival Program were already making a huge impact. As one of Compassion's website developers, I was excited to highlight these new programs online so our donors could see the impact their donations were having.

"Most donors will never get within three hundred miles of the poverty in Haiti, but if they can watch a video on their computer that gets them even three steps closer to a mom who lives it every day, then we will have done our job well," I said.

"You're passionate about this, aren't you?" David asked.

"I hear you're pretty passionate yourself," I replied, knowing David's long history of working on behalf of children. Though this was our first time working together, David had worked with Compassion many times before. I had reviewed his past work and was impressed with not only his camera skills and creativity but also his interest in helping children. Having worked with orphan ministries and other child-based advocacy programs, he was uniquely qualified to do this job.

Opening the creaky wooden door, I stepped right into the church sanctuary, where forty moms with babies and young children were waving their arms, singing, and clapping in time with the Creole rhythms. Some women turned their faces heavenward and closed their eyes as they lost themselves in the worship music. Others held babies with one arm and waved the other. Most were dressed in outdated Western clothes, their wardrobes the obvious remnants of donations received from mission teams of the past. A bright blend of colorful dresses and T-shirts moved and swayed in time to the music, contrasting with the dark interior of the solid concrete building and the sturdy gray benches that lined the center aisle. The room was more festive and alive than I had imagined while reading reports about the program before I left Colorado.

"I'm going to check the lighting," David said as we dropped the gear toward the back of the church. I left him to set up his equipment and joined Ephraim and Johnnie, who were already talking to the pastor in the opposite corner of the sanctuary.

"Thank you for coming," Pastor Yves said, giving me a hug. He didn't speak English so Johnnie translated for him. "We're glad you are here to tell our story."

I hoped I could.

Typically, my job at Compassion was to take existing photos and videos produced by others and present them online to tell stories about the work Compassion was doing all over the world. But this was the first time I was the one responsible for actually capturing the stories and images I would need. I had four days to find video that would move donors to care about mothers and babies they'd never met in places they'd never been. I knew David would help me put together an effective piece, but I was still nervous to do the actual interviews and serve as the creative director, making decisions about which stories and images to capture. A lot was riding on this, and I felt the weight of the responsibility.

I glanced over at David and watched as he studied the room, looking for natural sources of light. Once he found the right spot, he carefully set down his bags, opened the tripod, and adjusted it to the right height. Next he unpacked his gear, put batteries in the video camera and mics, and inserted a fresh tape. He checked the audio level and adjusted the settings, then nodded to let me know he was ready.

All of Compassion's child development programs are implemented through local churches. Compassion provides a comprehensive program and materials, while churches adapt the program for the needs of their communities. The last thing I wanted this church to do was stage anything for us; we wanted to capture their program exactly as they practiced it.

"Don't change a thing. We just want to observe," I told the pastor.

When the singing finished, the child survival specialist joined us after turning the group over to one of her helpers. We introduced ourselves, and, with her permission, I picked up my camera and started taking pictures of the women and their babies, giving David the nod to start filming.

The moms were seated on benches, listening to the leader. "Pick up your babies and talk to them. Let them stare at and touch your face. This will help them grow socially and emotionally." This was new information to many of these women. In a country where 80 percent of families live in extreme poverty, surviving on less than two dollars a day, babies are often parked in a corner of the house while mothers do what they can to provide for them. Interacting with their babies is something these mothers have never seen modeled.

I tried to remain unobtrusive, but being a white male in a remote Haitian church filled with women and children made that impossible. When the kids saw me, they stared with curiosity over the safety of their mothers' shoulders or from behind their skirts. The girls' beaded braids lightly jingled as they turned their heads to get a better look.

"To keep your baby healthy, remember to filter your water," the leader instructed. There was a sense of camaraderie, a bonding that took place among the women. I focused on their faces and tried to capture the joy in their expressions with my lens.

The leader invited a couple of people to join her at the front. Under her direction, they began a role-playing game. I was surprised to see there were also a few men participating. Why not? Fathers needed to learn these skills too. The men acted out a scene under the leader's direction, and there was give-and-take dialogue — a teasing banter between the group and the leader. The laughter was hearty and the mood was happy. The women seemed engaged — heart, mind, and soul — with the leaders and their lessons. The whole place throbbed with passion and energy.

I tried to get the little ones to smile as I took their pictures. Since I didn't speak the language, the best I could do was to try to engage them with simple mimes and oversized gestures. One boy cautiously stared at me. He was eating a piece of candy that was too big for his mouth. The candy dripped onto his lips and his mother's shirt. In an effort to get him to smile, I pretended to put candy in my mouth and chew it with exaggerated jaw movements. His eyes opened wide before he hid behind his mom's skirt. *Glad I don't make my living as a child photographer.* Fortunately, I was working with David; he was a natural with kids and could get them to smile at anything.

David finished filming group shots just as the day's instruction ended. I watched as he slipped his headphones off his head and slung them over the back of the camera. The hint of a smile on his face told me he was happy with the footage he'd taken. Dressed in a long-sleeved khaki shirt and dark cargo pants with a gray belt pack, David could almost have blended into the concrete-colored background, but his eyes were focused intently on the situation and his face reflected the gratification this kind of work brought him. David wasn't the kind of guy to demand a lot of attention, but he was so present in the situation you couldn't overlook his presence in the room.

Together we scouted the area for a background where we could do individual interviews with some of the mothers. Once we found a spot that would work well, I brought over white plastic chairs for the mothers to sit in while David moved his tripod, mounted the video camera, and adjusted the lighting. Then, one at a time, a few of the women came over and sat with their children in front of the camera for interviews. Ephraim took a backseat, content to let us do our jobs, but Johnnie offered lots of suggestions and was perfectly comfortable being at the center of everything. I gave Johnnie my list of interview questions, and he talked with the mothers, translating their answers while we filmed so I could make sure we had what we needed.

"What hopes and dreams do you have for your baby?" I asked through Johnnie.

The women smiled and their eyes sparkled as they answered this particular question.

"I want my boy to have a good job and to love God his entire life."

"Something I hope for is that my daughter finishes high school. No one in my family has done that."

"When my son grows up, he will be an architect."

I was surprised at their answers, because these were the same kinds of dreams I had for my boys. But in places with extreme poverty — places like Haiti — these dreams don't often come true. Yet these women had hope. Because of the help they received through Compassion, it was possible for their children to grow up happy and healthy, to get a job, and to live out their mothers' dreams.

"If people could just see these moms, they would want to partner in this process," I said.

"I feel that way every time I do one of these shoots," said David.

As David packed up his equipment, I went to thank Pastor Yves for his help. Ephraim and Johnnie were already engaged in conversation about local news and politics, though I didn't understand a lot of what was being said. As I approached, I saw the joy drain from Ephraim's face. His ever-present smile was replaced by dark shadows. He said something to the pastor, spitting out a word with such force I was caught off guard.

"What is *rest-o-veck*?" I asked.

"Restavek," Ephraim corrected me. "When parents sell their children."

Johnnie saw the horror on my face. "*Restavek* is a Creole word," he said. "It means 'stays with,' as in one who stays with a family though they are not a part of that family."

"Like a boarder?"

"No, like their slave." Ephraim's eyes held a deep sadness. "It's not for money. When the mothers sell their children, they do it because they believe someone else can offer their child a better life."

"Isn't that illegal?"

"Not in Haiti."

Through Johnnie, the pastor and Ephraim explained how restaveks are made to work long hours, are often underfed, and almost always abused — often sexually. Early intervention is the key to the prevention of more children becoming restaveks.

I thought of the babies on their mothers' hips and the toddlers hiding behind them. The girls with beaded braids. The boy with the candy that was too big for his mouth. The help and hope their mothers received meant these babies and toddlers would be spared that fate. As the photos I'd taken of the children flashed through my mind, I had a fresh understanding of why Compassion's work here was so important. I prayed a silent prayer that God would help me to tell the story in a way that would make a difference for all of Haiti's children.

———

After a short drive and a long walk from the church, we arrived at the home of one of the mothers in the Child Survival Program. As we approached, Missoul held down a section of the barbed-wire fence that encircled her concrete house. The barbed wire hardly seemed child-safe as Ephraim, Johnnie, David, and I stepped over it, and I could only imagine what dangers it protected her family from. Missoul and her three daughters were used to climbing in and out, but she held it down to safeguard her guests. Her efforts touched me.

She entered the house first and put her youngest daughter on the floor. Her house was small — smaller than a standard kitchen in the United States. It was made with the common elements of most Haitian slum houses, concrete blocks and a scavenged corrugated metal roof. It was designed to protect them from the elements and their most-feared natural disaster — a hurricane. Missoul had few furnishings. The only colors in the room were from the ripped sheets on her bed and the faded clothes that hung on nails in the walls because there were no chests or shelves. A campfire-type stove about a foot and a half wide sat on the floor in one corner of the room and served as the kitchen for her family of four.

Missoul had three daughters. The oldest girl had a big toothy smile and a sweet disposition, but it was obvious she had severe mental challenges. The second daughter was quiet and never smiled. She also had cognitive deficiencies, but they weren't as readily apparent.

It was the third and youngest sister who didn't seem to fit with the rest of the family. Just glancing at two-year-old Micheleine, I could see her health and intelligence. Her eyes engaged mine when I looked at her; she interacted with others and seemed to have more life energy than her two older sisters combined. It was clear that this was a loving family, but not one without problems.

The two oldest daughters faced challenges because of Missoul's malnutrition and lack of health care during her pregnancies. I knew that Missoul had also lost a baby during a previous pregnancy, and I wondered if I dared ask her about that loss.

During Missoul's fourth pregnancy, Compassion staff heard about her while making routine visits to the slums. They invited her to become a part of the program at Pastor Yves's church, which ensured she had proper nutrition and medical care both during her pregnancy and after the birth of her third daughter, Micheleine.

David unpacked his bags and set up the tripod, lights, and camera. He filmed Missoul as she described her life before and after Compassion's involvement. Not only were there improvements with her physical well-being; there were also spiritual changes. Though she continued to work as hard as she always had, now that she was a follower of Christ she had new hope for her life and for her family. She also felt the support of other mothers and of her church.

While we talked, Micheleine played on the floor near us. The older girls hung back, unsure of the strangers in their home. When the toddler grew restless, Missoul found an empty Coke can and dropped two small rocks inside. She shook it, enticing the little girl to reach for it. Micheleine stretched out her pudgy hand and grabbed it, smiling at the noise it made as she shook it. When Missoul leaned over and ran her fingers through toddler's hair, I smiled at her tenderness.

Missoul's face had a weathered look. It was hard to tell how old she was, but it was easy to see she had endured many hardships in her life. Her face was intense, almost hard, but the lines softened and melted away when she smiled, which she did rarely for strangers but often for her children.

During Missoul's last pregnancy, Compassion's Child Survival Program provided her with prenatal vitamins and health care. They educated her on nutrition for herself and for her baby. And after Micheleine's birth, Compassion's care through the church continued — teaching her proper child care and making it possible for her baby to be vaccinated. In Haiti, something as simple as a vaccination can change the trajectory of a child's life. Good health provides a distinct advantage for a future that can include education and an opportunity to find meaningful work. Because of early intervention, this toddler now had the potential to lift the whole family out of poverty.

I was encouraged to think that more than 2,500 Haitian moms and their babies were receiving similar care through this program, but thousands more still needed help. I hoped Missoul's readiness to share her story would help to motivate more people to get involved in the support of this ministry.

As the interview continued, whatever I lacked in creative direction, David made up for with his experience. He suggested we get some B-roll footage of her making the long trek from her house to her water source. As he directed Missoul, the neighbors laughed and teased her. I heard them pointing and calling Missoul a name that made Ephraim laugh. I looked at Johnnie.

"Movie star," he said.

David and I joined in the laughter. Then he caught my eye. "Do we have it?"

———

"We got it, David — we got the story! Anything else we get on this trip is gravy," I said once we were back in the SUV. We still had another mother to interview the next day, but it felt good knowing that no matter how that turned out, we had gotten what we'd come for. As I settled in my seat for the thirty-minute ride back to Port-au-Prince, the stress that had nagged me for weeks slipped away. I smiled to think that this was how God was choosing to use me right now, and I couldn't think of a better way to live out my faith. I hoped Missoul's story would impact others as much as it had me.

As we drove back toward Port-au-Prince, I watched as the sun revealed patterns of light and color on the ramshackle houses covering the hillsides. There were so many homes that they appeared to be stacked on top of each other like a large-scale game of Jenga. If one shifted, it looked as if they would all topple. These were the slums where so many of Haiti's poor lived. Our route took us past a few voodoo temples and reminded me of how desperate so many people were for hope. I wasn't in Colorado Springs anymore.

———

On the ride back to the hotel, I called my wife, Christy. Things have always been tight for us financially. Working at a nonprofit doesn't pay as well as a corporate job, so together we started a small Internet-based business. We depended on advertisers' checks to help pay our bills. I needed Christy to pick up one of those checks and deposit it before the bank closed, so it would clear in time to pay bills due at the end of the week. She answered on the first ring.

"Hi, honey. How was your day? Did you get the check picked up and deposited?"

"Yeah, I did it this morning." She talked about the kids and her plans for the day. "I won't go into all the details. I'll save that for when you get back. How do you like Haiti?"

"I wish you were here with me to experience this and meet the people. Haiti is a tropical paradise buried under poverty. There is so much beauty in the land and joy in the people that it would be easy to just look the other way and miss seeing the desperation in their living conditions. But the hardness and pain of poverty is always right there." As we rolled through the lush green countryside, my view from the SUV window confirmed my comment. "David and I are headed back to the hotel. We're pretty tired, so we'll probably lie down for a few minutes and get dinner after that." Christy and I said our good-byes, and I promised to call after dinner when I had more time to talk.

As we entered the outskirts of Port-au-Prince, Ephraim and Johnnie kept up a running dialogue of jokes and stories. They expressed frustration as they talked about Haiti's history and politics. From the backseat, I could see Ephraim's eyes in the rearview mirror. Though there was always joy on his face, his eyes reflected the deep stress of living in and around this poverty. All day, he'd been our biggest cheerleader, with nothing but enthusiasm for our work. But I could see flashes of frustration while he drove, especially when we passed children begging in the streets. Life in Haiti is anything but easy.

I grabbed my zoom lens and attached it to the camera hanging around my neck. As we entered the concrete-gray city, surges of color caught my photographer's eye: a woman's bright, fuchsia T-shirt; soft pastels on her daughter's jumper; vivid yellow stripes on a young boy's button-down shirt; piles of green bananas and stacks of red potatoes at roadside stands; black pigs and brown dogs wandering through emerald grass.

The most eye-catching of all were the flamboyant Haitian buses. Called tap-taps, these taxi-buses are rolling graffiti billboards, showcasing some of Haiti's most festive artwork. They were overfilled with people wearing tropical-colored prints on shirts, skirts, and headscarves. In Haiti, most buildings are gray, and poverty casts dark shadows. But the people of Haiti defy this bleakness with their artwork, laughter, and singing. The environment may be gray, but Haitian dreams are in living color.

We turned on to the steep and winding one-lane, quarter-mile road that led to the hotel, and several times I caught my breath as our car hugged a tight curve on the edge of a steep drop-off. I could see the shining white columns and the layered terraces that glimmered in the late afternoon sun as they clung to the side of the Hotel Montana. The open-air lobby, shaded portico, and tropical colors of the building were a welcome relief from the bleak architecture we'd passed on our way in.

Ephraim pulled into the roundabout in front of the hotel, put the SUV in park, and cut the engine. He opened the door, and as we exited the SUV, he first grabbed David, and then me, in a bear hug. *If there is one person who will remind me of Haiti when I get home, it will be Ephraim.* I made a mental note to take pictures with him tomorrow.

"Thanks, guys!" David said, unloading his equipment from the back of the SUV.

I glanced at my watch. It was 4:52. "We'll eat dinner in the hotel tonight and meet back here in the morning at — oh, how about eight o'clock?" I said to Johnnie. He conferred with Ephraim, who agreed.

They waved and started the engine.

I slung my backpack over my shoulder and followed David into the lobby.

Perhaps the nicest hotel in all of Haiti, the Hotel Montana has been called the crowning jewel of Port-au-Prince. From the terrace, you have stunning views of the mountains, the coast, and downtown Port-au-Prince. The vantage point made the hotel seem almost luxurious, despite the poverty that waited just down the hill. During times of political turmoil, it was considered one of the few safe places for foreigners to stay.

As we entered the lobby, the registration desk was directly ahead of us. The white pillars and colonnades reflected the bright afternoon sun, making the whole lobby area radiate with warmth and light. We turned left at the registration desk and headed toward the small elevators but at the last second decided to turn our backs to the lobby and instead take the outdoor stairway that led to our room. It would give us a chance to breathe in the warm Caribbean air and get one more look at the panoramic view.

We had only taken a step or two in the direction of the stairs when a boom shook the hotel like a fierce thunderclap might shake a house, but instead of windows rattling, the walls rippled as if they were made of liquid. I'm not sure I heard the boom so much as I *felt* it in my chest. The explosions continued one on top of another, near and far away, like the sounds of artillery on a battlefield.

3

BACK AGAINST THE WALL

Suddenly, loud explosions burst from every direction. I felt like we were in a war zone, and every bomb was aimed directly at us. The blasts were followed by the sounds of walls crashing and breaking. A wave of concrete ground unbalanced me as the floor shifted beneath my feet and I heard David's voice screaming confirmation of what I already knew.

"Earthquake!"

I had grown up in California and instinctively knew what was happening even before David said it. Like an air bag deploying in a car accident, adrenaline detonated inside my veins. Every muscle in my body poised to spring. With no doorjamb to jump into, and no desk or other large furniture to dive under or next to, the safest place seemed to be the staircase in front of me. I lunged toward it — toward the outdoors — and hopefully toward safety.

The intensity was unbelievable. The violent jerking twisted the hotel walls, severing columns and support beams, causing the walls to buckle and fall around us.

As I looked toward the outside stairs, I caught a glimpse of the brilliant blue sky visible through the open-air archway. I watched as the arch swayed and bowed before me, then broke and fell. I never made it to the stairs.

Instantly, the lobby went from vibrant color to black. I couldn't see anything. *Was I dead?* Something heavy fell near me. I was forced into a crouched position, with a fallen wall at my back and against my head, where just a blink of color ago there was no wall.

But I felt pain: it radiated from my leg to my head. I tried to take another step, but I couldn't. My left foot was pinned and trying to yank it free made the throbbing worse. The pain told me I wasn't dead.

Fear, or maybe bile, rose from my stomach to my throat.

Was I blind? I turned my head in every direction searching for light. I lifted my hand in front of my face and couldn't see it. A fine powder coated my face and collected in my nostrils, reminding me of demolitions I had done when I worked construction jobs. It smelled like concrete.

It smelled broken.

The explosive sounds were replaced by the thunder of concrete slabs falling and shattering as they pancaked on top of each other. There was screaming from places I couldn't see and voices I didn't recognize.

"Help!"

"Who's there? I need help!"

I added my own voice to the cacophony. "David!"

"I'm injured — can somebody help me?" I couldn't focus. I couldn't think. I feared for my life. The shaking and the sounds of destruction continued for much too long.

When the quake started, David had been to my left, but in the blackness I couldn't see him. I yelled again.

"David?"

Lord, please help me. Help me find David.

David didn't respond. Alone and pinned in place, I panicked. Each breath came faster but also harder. The dust collecting in my lungs left me gasping for air. I coughed. Between breaths, I continued to yell. I felt light-headed, but I couldn't stop. No longer was I controlling the yelling; it was controlling me.

"Please, God, help me and David!"

"DAAAAAA — VID!"

The noise decreased to a trickle of rubble. I had been blindly yelling, but I no longer heard my own voice. I stopped screaming. *Did I black out?* I couldn't have; though bent over, I was still on my feet, but I couldn't feel my backpack on my shoulder. *It must have been ripped off when the wall above me fell.*

I tried to make sense of my surroundings. My senses were on heightened alert, making my inability to see even more alarming. *Had I been blinded by an injury or just the dust?* I reached frantically in every direction, trying to feel for something, anything — but I grasped only air and the fallen wall behind my head.

"Ephraim! Johnnie? Is anybody there?"

Something altered in my mind. I had been desperately crying out to God — to anyone who would help. But now calm swept over me. The feelings of panic and desperation suddenly vanished, and I was left with only a dull dread that settled in my stomach. It was hard to understand. It's not that I wasn't afraid; I was. But it was as if God cleared my mind so I could focus. Though my muscles relaxed, my mind felt as sharp and tense as my body had a few minutes earlier when I lunged toward the stairs.

Pain seared the back of my head, and when I reached to check it, I got a handful of blood. I knew it could be serious, but I also knew that even minor head wounds bled heavily. My breaths were quick and shallow. I could feel my heart race. But I observed those things from a detached perspective, as if I was analyzing someone else in a crisis situation.

I knew I needed to move to a safer place. There would be aftershocks, and some of them would be big. But moving anywhere wasn't going to be easy. My head throbbed, and I felt nauseous. *Think. You've got to think about what to do next.*

My leg was pinned by something I couldn't see. In the darkness, I reached down and felt a piece of concrete six to eight inches long, and I heaved it to the side. That cleared a space so I could move the other pieces of concrete and wood debris and dig a hole large enough to free my foot. But even then it didn't come out easily. I lost my left shoe when I yanked my foot loose. I reached down to grab the shoe, but it wouldn't budge. I'd watched enough survival shows to know that shoes could be vital in surviving an earthquake, so I tried again. Despite my best efforts, I still couldn't get it.

As I stood up, I felt something bump against my chest. My camera! It was still around my neck. Fumbling in the dark, I felt for the button to turn it on, and then I saw the small display screen light up. *I'm not blind!* I pushed down the shutter, and a small light from the autofocus flashed for a split second. *I can use this. Thank you, God!* In order to see, I flashed the light and then tried to form a mental picture of what I'd just seen. In the pitch-black it wasn't much, but it was better than being blind.

Using my new method of "seeing" in the dark, I tried to look around. What I thought was the wall against my back was actually the ceiling. One side had fallen behind me while a portion of it remained precariously perched against the wall in front of me, forming a sort of lean-to above me. This created the open pocket where I now crouched. Looking at it, I realized that I'd escaped being crushed by mere inches. *How had this space stayed intact while the six stories above it collapsed?*

Each time I put weight on my left side, the pain was unbearable. *My leg must be broken.* I pointed the camera toward my leg to examine my injury. The flash of light revealed that my khakis were soaked in blood. *Oh, great; I survived the earthquake, but now my leg could do me in!* I couldn't feel where the break was, so I tried to stand on my right foot as much as possible while I looked for a safe place to treat my wounds.

With each breath I inhaled more dust. It was so thick I could chew it. The sounds of rubble falling had lessened. So had the cries for help. But the threat wasn't over. I still needed to get somewhere safe. If the ceiling slipped or the wall that held it up fell, it was likely they both would come down. Using the focus light of the camera, I tried to scan my surroundings, but without my glasses, what I saw wasn't very helpful. Doing the best I could, I flashed the light and tried to remember what I saw.

One of the supporting beams that had held up the ceiling was down in front of me. It was about three feet off the ground at its highest point and rested against the wall; it was cracked and breaking in the middle. The whole thing looked as if it could slip at any time. There was nothing safe about this lobby. Before the earthquake, the lobby ceiling was a huge concrete slab held up by pillars that propped up five more stories of the same. Now all of that had collapsed, and I was at the bottom of it. I knew that any structural integrity that remained could fail.

I used the camera to take a picture of the joint where the ceiling met the wall. Examining it on the small screen confirmed my fears. It was cracking and breaking and looked as if it could easily give way if the pressure shifted.

I crouched down and lowered the camera to take a picture from underneath the toppled support beam. On the small preview screen, I saw what appeared to be a shower. *That doesn't make any sense.* I turned off the camera to think. *That's not a shower; that's the elevator!* I turned the camera back on and studied the picture.

It was definitely the elevator. Not only was the elevator car at lobby level; its door was stuck open. *What a miracle!* Though I knew elevators weren't safe during an earthquake because they could fall, this one couldn't go any lower. The elevator car was a self-contained box with reinforced sides, and the shaft where it resided didn't share walls with the lobby. The elevator would offer the best protection, not only from falling debris, but also from a total collapse of the remaining hotel walls.

There was one big problem. To get to the elevator, I needed to crawl over a pile of rubble and under the broken support beam. While the beam appeared stable, I could see cracks and knew there was a lot of weight pushing down on it from above. At any moment it could break in half. If I were under it when that happened, at best, I'd be trapped. At worst; well, I knew what the worst was. *Should I risk crawling under it?*

Whatever I decided, I had to act now.

4

TREMORS

April 1993

Azusa, California

"I feel like I want to hurt myself."

Her words stunned me. Nothing could have prepared me for a call like this from my beautiful, bright-eyed fiancée. I struggled to understand what she said.

There was a lot going on. College graduation was just weeks away, and our wedding would follow shortly after that. End-of-semester projects, studying for finals, and wedding plans had kept both of us on the go. It made sense that Christy felt tired, stressed, overwhelmed, and maybe a little sad. There were big changes ahead in our future.

For weeks, I'd noticed that she seemed down. I thought it was just an emotional swing that would fade away. But wanting to hurt herself? I had no way of wrapping my mind around that. Why would she want to harm herself?

I wouldn't say I am a naive optimist, but I tend to have a "glass half full" approach to life. I don't ignore problems; I just think most of them are solvable. *But how do I solve this?*

"Dan, I'm scared."

"Christy, you're going to be OK. I'll be right over. Will you be safe until I get there?"

"Yes."

"I'll be there in two minutes!" I hung up the phone, grabbed my keys, and started running across campus.

I remembered the first day I met Christy Schroeder three years earlier. She was new to Azusa Pacific University but was already using her leadership skills on campus. She asked if I would help her organize a campus prayer meeting for Halloween night. She had the brightest smile. When we talked, her dark brown eyes stared so intently into mine it was as if my spoken words weren't enough. She seemed to want to penetrate my thoughts. I was flattered. And it didn't hurt that she was cute — really cute! Her dark blonde shoulder-length hair curled in ringlets around her milky white face. I enjoyed her attention and was excited to work on a project with her. Over the next two years, Christy and I became best friends and fell in love.

Christy was free with her emotions, and I loved that. If there was something to celebrate, I wanted Christy there. If I were sad, Christy would be sad with me. She was the best person to share emotions with because she fully engaged her sensitive heart. My emotional expressions tended to be very controlled, but when I was with Christy, her highs energized me and her lows brought out my protective, nurturing side. I needed her emotional range to help me experience the fullness that life offered.

As I crossed the field in front of the administration building, I tried to make sense of the situation. I really didn't think Christy would hurt herself. I wanted to believe this was just an example of her expressive emotions. But Christy had never made a call like this before. I had to take her words seriously — in case thoughts of hurting herself led to something worse, like thoughts of suicide.

I knew from experience how tragic suicide was for the loved ones left behind. It had forever changed my family. My aunt and grandfather had both committed suicide, and then my mother took her own life before I turned two.

My dad remarried when I was three, and my stepmother was the only person I ever called Mom. Growing up, I heard distant references to and stories about my birth mother, but I didn't understand why she left. It just wasn't something we talked about. Back then, we called my mother's disorder "manic depression" (now it's known as bipolar disorder), but at the time I was too young to know what that meant, what caused it, or why someone would get depressed in the first place.

As Christy's building came into view, I realized I had no idea how to help her. I knocked on her door, and without waiting for a response, I let myself in. The apartment was dark. The late-afternoon sun had dropped behind the campus buildings, casting long shadows on the residence hall, and Christy hadn't yet turned on a light. She sat on the floor in the middle of her apartment, wearing old sweats. I'd seen her cry before, but she looked different this time. Her once-bouncy ringlets were disheveled and hung limply. She hadn't showered or washed her hair. Sweat and tears glued the matted curls to her face. The cordless phone lay on the floor next to an empty box of Kleenex — the pile of used tissues told me she'd been there for a long time.

When she looked up, I saw her puffy, red eyes. They startled me. There was a sense of fear, maybe even panic, in them I'd never seen before.

"I'm here. It's OK." I slowly walked to the middle of the room and knelt in front of her. She got on her knees, wrapped her arms around my neck, and pressed herself into my chest. I hugged her tighter as sobs racked her body. "Shhh, it's going to be OK." I held her and kissed her. "I'm here, Sweet; it's OK." After the initial wave of sobbing passed, her crying subsided, replaced by quiet tears that fell freely onto my shoulder. I could still feel her body trembling, but she seemed to be gaining control.

I wasn't a therapist. I'd never had any kind of training for such a situation, so I tried to think of what a counselor might say. "Can you tell me what you're feeling?"

"I'm scared, Dan. I am so scared." Her face was still buried against my chest, and I had to listen closely to hear her muffled words.

"What are you afraid of, honey?"

"I keep picturing in my head ways I could hurt myself." She looked up at me.

Her brown eyes betrayed fears she couldn't articulate, fears I couldn't understand. I wanted to dive into her eyes and not come out until I had chased away all her pain. I didn't know what to say next, but I felt I needed to keep her talking. "Have you tried anything?"

"No."

I exhaled slowly and paused slightly before asking, "What do you mean when you say 'hurt yourself'?"

"I don't know. I just keep having these horrible thoughts."

Her breathing slowed, and the crying dissipated. She was becoming more responsive to me and interacting more.

I didn't need to remind her of all the stress she was under — potential causes of this crisis — but I did anyway. In addition to all the wedding planning and our upcoming graduation, she was having health issues. To cure a rare blood infection, her doctor had prescribed some strong medications and eliminated all dairy, fruit, and grains from her diet. As she planned and attended end-of-the-year parties and events for the residents in her living area, she was unable to eat most of the foods. She had amazing willpower, but the restrictive diet was taking an emotional toll on her ability to let loose and have fun. It also affected her physically. She had lost weight, and her hair had started to thin.

"You've been so stressed and so tired."

"I know," she said. She curled into a ball in my lap, rested her head against my chest, and closed her eyes.

"You know that I am here for you, right? You can call me anytime. I'll always help you through whatever you're feeling."

"I know."

"Christy, I can't let anything happen to you."

"Uh-huh."

I asked her to promise that if she ever had thoughts like these again, we would talk about them. If I wasn't around, or if she really thought she would act on her fears, she would get help immediately — even if that meant calling 911. She agreed.

Pressed against mine, her body quieted. As she rested in my lap, I could still hear an occasional sniffle. I sensed the crisis had passed.

As I ran my fingers through her damp hair, I felt a catch in my throat and tried to hold it back. My chest tightened, my stomach contracted, and the tears started flowing freely. Christy sat up and looked at me. I buried my face in my hands and cried harder.

"Are you OK?" She tried to console me, but I could no longer respond.

Our roles had reversed. My crying turned to uncontrollable sobbing. My chest heaved, my nose ran, and I didn't care who heard me. It came from deep inside of me; from a place I had never been. I was twenty-three years old, crying like a two-year-old who'd just lost his mother.

I finally gained enough control to speak. "I'm sorry. I'm so sorry. I don't know what that was," I said as I tried to get my breath back. By now, my head was pounding and my chest hurt. Then I said what I'd really wanted to say all night, "I'm so afraid of losing you. Please don't ever leave me through suicide."

Christy stroked my face. Her hand felt cool against my sweaty skin, and I leaned into her embrace. She looked deep into my eyes and gently probed, "Dan, something else is upsetting you. What's really wrong?"

I took a few minutes to consider my response.

"I'm crying for my mother."

Christy held me for a few minutes, and the wave of crying subsided.

I needed a tissue, and I stood to go to the bathroom. Christy held up her hands, and I pulled her up next to me. We hugged and walked together to the bathroom. I grabbed a Kleenex and passed one to her, and we both blew our noses, loudly, at the same time.

She started to giggle, and I laughed. We stood side by side in front of the mirror, blowing our red noses. I couldn't help thinking how unattractive we both looked with our blotchy, swollen faces. "Wanna go out for dinner?" I asked.

She laughed, and I saw the smile I fell in love with.

We stayed in and had takeout, spending a quiet evening on the couch with a rented movie. Before I left that night, I reminded her again of her promise.

"We're a team; we'll make it through together," I said, pressing my lips against hers.

My initial fears had subsided, and as I left, I felt as though she wasn't in any imminent danger. Not that I was qualified to make that judgment, but to me, her symptoms seemed more like extreme stress, situational depression, or perhaps an overactive imagination. We'd both cried — a lot, which was probably good — and now we would be fine. She had even helped me through some hidden pain I wasn't aware of. Episode closed.

I said a quick prayer for Christy, "Dear Father, please be with her and keep her safe."

By the time I reached my apartment, I had already started to doubt the pep talk I had given myself. In bed, my last thought before I fell asleep was, *I'd better keep my eye on this.*

5

LIFE-CHANGING DECISIONS

Tuesday Afternoon

Hotel Montana, Port-au-Prince

Aftershocks were likely at any moment, and I needed to make a choice. If I stayed where I was, I risked the ceiling slipping down the wall and crushing me. But I didn't like the idea of ducking under the already cracked support beam either. I pictured it breaking in two and crushing me as I crawled under. Either way, I was in a precarious situation. I looked again at the photos on my camera, paying special attention to the image of the joint where the fallen ceiling met the wall. I didn't have to study it for long. It looked like it could go any second. I needed to move.

Because there were only a few feet between the beam and the debris below it, I would have to crawl on my belly. I also knew that if I decided to go for it, there would be no turning back. As soon as I put my head under the beam, I was committed to come out on the other side — or die trying. But dragging my bad leg through the debris on the floor would be painful and difficult. *What happens if I start the crawl and can't finish it?* I took one last look at the joint and decided it was too risky to stay. I knew if I didn't get out of the pocket, I would die there.

If I'm going to die, I want to die doing everything I can to get home to my family.

I took a deep breath and squatted lower, wincing at the pain in my leg. I pushed the camera around to my back, tucked my head under the beam, and pushed off with my right leg. Lying on my stomach and using my elbows, I began to army-crawl through the rough pieces of concrete, torn metal, and shards of glass.

The pain hit my torso first. Though I had on two shirts — a black T-shirt with a dark gray button-down on top of it — I could still feel the sharp rubble tearing at my chest as I crawled. My arms had been injury free but soon gathered their own battle scars. My left leg burned like fire as chunks of debris scraped my wounds through the rip in my pants. While dragging my useless leg across the floor, I could feel even the smallest pieces ripping into the bloody lesion. But I didn't care about the increased pain. It was a good distraction; I momentarily forgot my fear as I swiftly worked my body, inch by inch, through the wreckage.

The darkness made it hard to tell how far I'd gotten, but when I thought I'd cleared the beam, I slowly pushed up to a kneeling position. I flashed the camera again and found that I was in a pocket very similar to the one I had just left, though this one was larger. Two elevators were straight ahead of me, and the door on the left car — the one in the picture I had taken — was open. I stood up slowly. The pain in my left leg made me dizzy. *Something's broken.* I balanced my weight on my right leg, then quickly hobbled through the open door and into my new home.

I made it!

Groping around in the dark, I found the elevator car to be about the size of a shower stall. Attached to the back of the elevator, about waist high, was a handrail. The floor was layered with debris — broken chunks of concrete ranging from small stones to medium-sized chunks, but other than that I couldn't feel any other distinguishing features. I leaned against the wall to catch my breath and immediately felt the vibrations of an aftershock. It was a big one, nearly the size of the original quake. I grabbed the bar to balance myself but fell to the floor as the shaking, then jerking, increased. Something in the lobby outside of the elevator crashed, followed by the sounds of more falling debris. *How close was that? If I'd stayed out there, I could be dead right now.*

In the past few minutes, I'd come close to death twice. A verse from the Psalms came to mind: "God is my refuge and strength, an ever-present help in trouble." *Thank you, God, for being my refuge.*

———

The shaking stopped, and I swallowed the ball of fear that threatened to choke me. I had to figure out what to do next.

My iPhone!

As I reached my hand into my pocket, I could feel the familiar curved case of the battery cover I kept attached to the phone. I pulled it out. The phone felt smooth and cool. I had to be careful not to drop it. My hands were shaking as I felt for the On button. I fingered the phone's flat screen and could tell it hadn't cracked. I prayed that the phone still worked as my thumb found the familiar round button and pushed it. The screen lit up: 5:02, Tuesday, January 12 — less than ten minutes since the earthquake.

I checked for a signal, though I didn't expect to find one. I tried sending Christy a text message, but it wouldn't send. No signal. I stood up and limped around the elevator and even lifted the phone above my head. A gap over a foot wide was visible where the elevator car separated from the shaft above me. Shining the phone into the gap, I could see the shaft appeared to go up at least a few stories. I held my phone into the shaft to see if I could get the signal bars to light up. Nothing. I put the phone away. I guessed that every cell tower in Port-au-Prince was probably down, but I also knew cell towers would be among the first pieces of infrastructure to be restored. I wanted to save my battery so I could try later when I had a better chance of receiving a signal.

In the excitement over finding my phone, I hadn't paid much attention to my leg. But the pain told me I'd put more weight on it than I should have, and I was quickly losing blood. I knew I needed to treat my wounds immediately.

Moving the biggest pieces of debris to one side, I found a small spot where I could sit down with my back against the wall. In this position, I could extend my legs completely inside the car.

Debris continued to fall outside the elevator. It wasn't the loud explosive sounds I heard earlier, but more like the creaking and groaning that ice-covered tree limbs make before breaking off. I imagined pieces of debris falling from stories above me and gathering speed down the shaft before reaching the front of my car and slicing off my feet. I made a mental note to make sure I was always completely contained within the car.

Sitting wasn't comfortable. I felt chunks of concrete and rubble on the floor beneath me. I grimaced as I reached down and removed my left sock, which was saturated with blood. Using the camera light, I looked for injuries on my foot, but there was so much blood that I couldn't identify where the wound was. I pulled up my ripped and blood-covered left pant leg and examined my wounds.

OK, how bad can this be?

Flashing my camera again, I saw the gash on the inside of my leg. It ran from my knee to just above my ankle and was split wide-open. Inside the cut I could see a grisly, yellowed, cottage cheese–like substance. *Oh, this is bad!* I hadn't seen what had cut my leg and wondered if a broken bone had ripped it apart from the inside. Blood flowed freely from the opening. I knew I needed to apply pressure to stop the bleeding. *Should I also apply a tourniquet?*

I'd survived an earthquake; I didn't want to die from not treating my injuries properly. I wished I could recall more of my first aid training from years ago. Then I remembered, *I have an app for that!*

The guys at work teased me. They call me an appaholic for all the apps I download "just in case." But I had downloaded a first aid app to my iPhone because of Christy. As a mom, she's always prepared. She'd even insisted on putting together first aid kits for my car and office. I flicked through the screens until I found the app and then searched it for information to treat my injuries. Fortunately the app didn't need to connect to the Internet. All of the information was already downloaded onto my phone, so the response was quick: "Excessive Bleeding: Apply constant pressure." No mention of a tourniquet.

I took off my outer shirt and tried to tear it into strips to wrap around my leg, but I couldn't get the shirt to rip, so I wrapped the whole shirt around my leg. I hoped the pressure would stop the bleeding and keep any broken bones in place, but I needed something to secure it. I remembered seeing some insulated wire in the corner of the elevator that had been exposed by the quake. Using my fingers to feel and the light from my phone to see, I searched the elevator until I found the wire and ripped it from the wall. Then I tied it around the shirt to hold it in place. I prayed it would work.

I touched my head again. Although it was still bleeding, the flow seemed to have slowed. I removed my right shoe and sock and folded the sock to use as a compress on my head; then I put my shoe back on. I put the sock between my head and the wall, and then pressed my head hard against the sock so I could apply pressure without having to hold it in place.

Aftershocks continued. Some were intense; some were not. But I felt relatively safe inside of the elevator. I realized I had several things in my favor. I'd found safe shelter six stories under an earthquake-ravaged hotel. I had successfully treated my wounds, and I set the alarm on my iPhone to rouse me if I fell asleep. I knew God had protected me and helped me think clearly, and I had tools I could work with. *But would these things be enough?* What if the aftershocks got worse? I had lost a lot of blood, and I grew concerned about my ability to continue thinking straight.

The debris had mostly stopped falling, and things around me were still. I could occasionally hear voices in the distance. I strained to hear what they said, but it was too hard to make out the words.

It was comforting to hear other voices, but I wished one of them was David's. *Maybe he's just unconscious.* I replayed the scene in my mind, and I remembered how close we'd been standing when the wall came down. There was so much confusion, but I was pretty sure

David was less than three feet away from me. He was moving toward the stairs with me, which meant he would have been —

I pushed the thought out of my mind. *He's just unconscious*, I told myself.

Dear God, please save David. Let him just be unconscious. And whatever happens to him, please protect his family. As I prayed for them, I thought about my own wife and kids.

Christy.

I thought about her smile, and the smile in her eyes. In college, we were best friends before we fell in love. Once we did, I never doubted she was my soul mate. Sure, we had differences: I kept my emotions checked; Christy let hers splash all over — but I loved that she felt so free to express herself. We shared so much — our faith and values and our perspective on life. We loved exploring the world around us and then having long conversations about what we experienced. While Christy's depression could have torn our marriage apart, it had actually brought us closer together. I was so blessed to have her as my wife.

It had been too long since I had spent time thinking about the things I liked about Christy. I knew she had felt a chill between us lately. *How had we let that happen?*

I pictured her at home doing science experiments with our son Josh. Josh is our oldest, and though he is only six, I already feel proud of the young man he is becoming. He is smart — no doubt due in part to Christy's homeschooling — and funny, energetic, and kind. For his age, he is also very aware of spiritual things. I love to hear him talk about his desire to help others and to please God. I thought of his thick, wavy hair and big excited eyes as he would look up at me and say, "Let's build something, Dad!"

I thought of our three-year-old, Nathan. While the first thing everyone seems to notice is his cute blond ringlets, I'm more taken by his fearless personality. He embraces every experience full body and soul. His heart is as big as he is. "I love you as big as the whole wur-old!" he says, as he bear-hugs me with his chubby little arms. Sometimes he nearly chokes me — he is much stronger than he looks.

I missed my boys and I missed my girl and I knew they missed me — we needed each other. Sitting in my black pit, spitting out the dirt that still coated my mouth, one thought motivated me: *I had to live.*

6

READY TO DIE

Hotel Montana, Port-au-Prince

In Haiti, with the poverty and lack of preparation for a tragedy the magnitude of this earthquake, being rescued would take a miracle. Surviving my injuries would take another one. Though they were the outcomes I desperately wanted, as time passed, I knew the chances of both happening were slim. I had lost a lot of blood; there was no food or water; and the aftershocks continued. I tried to postpone my death in every way I could, but I knew very little was up to me.

Am I ready to die?

The answer was no.

I thought of my family — Christy and the boys. I didn't feel my life with them was finished. I didn't believe that my work, my purpose, and other relationships in my life were complete.

My faith as a Christian is an important part of who I am, of my essence. Though outwardly most who knew me would probably have thought of me as a strong Christian, I knew that I had allowed my heart to cool toward God in recent years. In the face of death and eternity, I could not lie to myself. Something in my soul, in the core of my being, was off-kilter, and I knew it.

God is the creator of the universe — of stars, of giraffes, of the Rocky Mountains that I see on my way to work every morning.

Yet it had been a long time since I had sincerely worshiped him or expressed wonder at his amazing works.

I believed he had created me with a specific purpose in mind, and I called him the Lord of my life, yet for how long had I made my own plans and managed the details of my life without involving him? How often did I seek his guidance and direction — really ask, and then wait for an answer? Who was in the driver's seat of my life? When was the last time I had spent any significant time — more than a few minutes — in prayer, in reading Scripture, in talking with others about God's work in our lives? Did I even miss it?

And if I was truly a Christ-follower, why did I so often make choices that didn't honor him? How much of the energy of my life — my time, my effort, my thoughts, my relationships — was dedicated to God's purposes? I was living a pretty standard, mediocre Christian life. My heart was lukewarm — neither hot nor cold toward God.

I wondered if God embraced and welcomed into heaven people like me, people who give lip service to their Christian faith without full-heart devotion. How could God say to me, "Well done, good and faithful servant," when for some time I had lived as if he weren't really important? If I really believed that the Creator God loved me, shouldn't my life be more than this?

I didn't know the answers to those questions, but I knew I didn't want to be that kind of Christian — a follower of Christ in name but barely in reality. I had never wanted to be that kind of person. I wanted to be someone whose heart was fully aligned with God's heart, with his purposes. A person whose natural response to the Creator God was worship, obedience, and a deep hunger for his presence. Someone who was motivated by Jesus' death on a cross to fight sin in my life and to serve others sacrificially. I longed to live my life in a consistent posture of devotion and surrender to God that bears fruit in my life.

How far I had come from who I used to be! Yes, I still believed — but why was there so little evidence in my heart and in my day-to-day existence? Why had I walked away from God in so many ways after all he had done for me through the years? And why had it taken an earthquake and a staring contest with death to see the problem?

So I prayed. I prayed an intense prayer, sincere to the core of my heart. I confessed sins, chief of all that I had abandoned the love and devotion that had once been the foundation of my spiritual life.

I surrendered my will and the plans I had for my life, and I asked God to make me his person again, no matter what came next. If that meant death, I asked him to accept me into heaven.

I expressed my love and gratitude to God for creating me, for sending Jesus to die for my sins, for accepting me as his child, and for all of the blessings he had given me in my life.

And then I let my tears flow. I worshiped and praised the God who understood the vastness of the universe yet does not fail to notice the falling of a sparrow. The God who knew about this moment in my life even before I was born.

And while I worshiped and prayed, I heard a voice in my head say:

You are mine!

In that moment, I realized that God had been pursuing me. He had pursued me to the bottom of this collapsed hotel because he wanted a deeper love relationship with me — he wanted *all* of me. Peace flooded over me, peace like I hadn't experienced for a long, long time. I knew that God held my future in his hands, whether that future was on earth or in heaven.

———

Sitting in one place for any length of time became unbearable. But every time I shifted positions, I stirred up dust and created new bits of gravel that clung to me and dropped into the area I had just cleared.

I heard others calling for help and decided to join in. I sucked in a deep breath and let it out. "Help! Helllllp! I'm injured!" I could really scream when I wanted to.

"We're over here. Can you help us?" It sounded as though his voice was coming from behind the fallen ceiling in front of the elevator.

"No, I'm trapped too."

"Where are you?" he asked.

"I'm in the elevator. Where are you?"

"We're trapped …" I listened hard, but I couldn't make out every word he said. "… lobby … next to the front desk."

"How many of you are there?"

"Five of us … trapped in a pocket that's only three feet tall … worried we might run out of air. Is anyone else with you?"

"No, I'm all alone." I wondered if *I* had enough air. It sounded like I was trapped in a much larger space than they were, but I didn't know how quickly air could be used up. The thought of suffocating, or hearing them suffocate, really scared me.

"Can you move around?" the voice asked.

"Uh, there's a bit of room in the lobby, but it's not really safe for me to leave the elevator."

"Don't do anything that isn't safe, but we were hoping you could come help us."

"I'm sorry. I can't get to you. I'm completely closed in by concrete walls."

"Oh." There was a pause as he relayed my answers to other survivors near him. "Can you see any light?"

"No, it's totally black."

I could hear him telling the others what I said. I listened as they got quiet. I knew it wasn't what they wanted to hear. From the sounds of things, they seemed to be in a more desperate situation than I was.

After a long pause, I returned to my thoughts. Describing my situation out loud to another person caused the peace from my prayer time to wear off and the fear to return. Though I knew I had gotten my heart right with God, I still didn't feel ready for my life on earth to be finished. I didn't want this to be my time to go, and I wondered how God would take care of my family if I didn't make it.

As my anxiety increased, I realized how vulnerable my thoughts were to severe swings toward despair. This was a big problem since I knew that my mental and emotional state could make a difference in my chances for survival. Panic often led to flawed judgment and mistakes. Despair could weaken my health. On the positive side, hope and the will to fight would keep my mind sharp and give me strength. I would have to keep a close watch on my thoughts and intentionally work to keep my hope alive.

I sang softly to try to calm my nerves.

"What's your name?"

It was the man's voice again. I wasn't sure if he could hear me singing or if he was just continuing the conversation. "I'm Dan. Daniel Woolley." I could hear him repeat the name to some of the people who were with him, but it sounded like he said "Dan Healy."

"My name's Jim. Jim Gulley. Are you injured, Dan? I'm keeping a list of names and injuries."

"I have a large cut on my leg, and I think it's broken. I also have a cut on my head, but it doesn't seem too bad. What about you?"

"There are five of us together. Myself, Rick, Ann, Clint, and Sam. Three of us have minor injuries, but Clint and Sam have their legs pinned. They're in a lot of pain." Jim explained that they were all Americans working for two different relief agencies — Interchurch Medical Assistance and the United Methodist Committee on Relief. They had met at the hotel for a dinner meeting. "And there's Sarla," said Jim. "She's not in the same space, but she's near us. She can move around some. We're hoping she can make contact with the outside world."

The concrete walls dampened his voice and at times muted the conversation. It was hard to catch everything he was saying, but it was heartening to not be completely alone. I hoped that having more people near me would increase the chances of us being rescued.

I could barely hear the others with Jim when they talked. Their voices didn't travel as well as his deep voice, and some of them sounded weakened by their injuries. But at least I could hear Jim; he seemed to be leading most of the conversations anyway. He'd repeat what I told him and then repeat back to me what they said.

"Describe to me where you are."

I told Jim about the lobby and how the ceiling and walls had fallen, creating the pocket outside of the elevator. I described the elevator and how the shaft had twisted away from the car. "I might be able to crawl up the elevator shaft and follow that to wherever it goes."

I could hear Jim talking excitedly to the others, telling them of the possibility. I tried to recall what I had seen when I had flashed the light from the camera up the shaft.

"Can you be safe doing it? What about your leg?"

"I'm not sure. I need to think about it some more."

Our conversation was interrupted by another aftershock. Though it wasn't as strong as the initial aftershocks, I still had to brace myself against the elevator wall to keep from falling over. With the jerking, chunks of debris from the elevator floor bumped against my injured leg, causing shooting pains. I hung on, gritting my teeth until the shaking stopped.

When things settled down, I thought again about climbing up the elevator shaft. While it might be possible, it would be very dangerous, especially with my injuries and the pain. Jim was right to raise concerns. For the time being, I shelved my Spiderman fantasy of scaling the shaft; even so, I wouldn't give up on the idea of finding a way out of this black abyss.

7

FROM ABOVE

My leg injury was without a doubt the worst I'd ever sustained in my life. I'd bound the gash with my shirt, but now the fabric was scraping against the open flesh — shifting in and out of the wound — whenever I moved my leg. Pieces of debris were still stuck in the lesion, and I could feel them rubbing against the ripped muscles and torn tissues inside my leg. The pain was constant and increased significantly when I moved. I tried to remain in one position for as long as I could. Despite the severity of the injury, the pain was more tolerable than I would have expected.

"Dan, what brings you to Haiti?" asked Jim.

I almost laughed at how normal this question sounded. It was as if we were just meeting each other casually in the hotel lobby under normal circumstances.

"I work for Compassion International with their Child Survival Program. I'm here to get stories of Haitian moms and babies on video so we can share them on our website."

We discussed our respective jobs and the work our organizations did for the poor. Jim occasionally paused to relay the details of our conversation to the others with him.

A sound from above startled me. *What was that?*

"Did you hear that?" I asked Jim.

"Hear what?"

"It sounded like a scraping noise." It was unlike anything I had yet heard. It seemed to come from above me, but I couldn't pinpoint the location. I could hear something sliding, but as I focused on the sound I realized it didn't have the same randomness I was used to hearing when the rubble shifted.

"It almost sounds as though someone is moving around or moving chunks of concrete." I tried to wrap my mind around what could be causing the odd sounds.

" … someone or something?" I only caught the last part of what Jim said but I could guess what he was thinking — because I was thinking it too.

Were rescuers trying to dig us out?

Only a few hours had passed since the quake. To be digging us out so quickly, someone needed to know we were here and exactly where to look for us. Who would know we were here?

Ephraim! And Johnnie! They'd just dropped David and me off at the hotel when the quake hit. They would have seen the building collapse. Were they trying to dig us out? If so, we had a very real chance of being rescued.

There was a pause followed by silence — it was as if he was listening for the sound of my voice. "Ephraim! Ephraim!" I shouted louder, but still no response. "Johnnie! Johnnie, is that you?"

"Dan, what's going on?" It was Jim again.

"It sounds like there's someone above me."

The work continued. I heard several large thuds — as if someone were pounding on walls near me.

"Do you think it could be a rescuer?"

"I don't know. Our translator and our driver had just dropped us off in front of the hotel before the quake hit. I'm thinking it could be them."

I cupped my hands around my mouth and yelled in different directions, attempting to target my voice toward the sounds. In the dark, it was hard to know where the noise originated. "Hello! Anyone there?"

I heard someone reply in a language I didn't understand. "Ephraim? Ephraim, is that you?"

At this point, I was convinced there was a person responsible for the noises. But as my confidence in the possibility of a real person increased, my confidence that it was *two* people decreased proportionally.

"Is it your guys?" Jim asked. I could hear the hopeful tone in his voice.

"Help! We need help!" I ignored Jim's question because I could tell that whoever was moving around was very close. "Can you hear me?"

"Helll-ooo?" The voice was definitely Haitian, but it wasn't Ephraim or Johnnie.

"We need help," I yelled. "Are you a rescuer?"

"What?"

I quickly assessed that while the man near me spoke some English, I'd have to simplify the things I said so he would understand me. "Can you help us?"

"No."

"Are you trapped?"

"Yes!"

I let out a slow breath. While it was encouraging to hear from other survivors, it was disappointing to find out that it wasn't Ephraim. Or Johnnie. Worst of all, it *wasn't* a rescuer.

"What is your name?" he asked.

"I'm Daniel."

"Hell-o, Dan-yell! I am Lukeson, I work in da hotel. Where are you, Dan-yell?"

"I'm in the elevator."

"I'm in da elevator too! I come to be with you."

I couldn't figure out where exactly Lukeson was. He said he was in the elevator. Was he in the shaft above me? Was he in the elevator shaft next to mine? I realized that my sense of direction must be very confused in the darkness.

"Dan, who is it?" I could hear the impatience in Jim's voice; he obviously heard my half of the conversation but not Lukeson's. I explained to Jim that it wasn't a rescuer but a member of the hotel staff, who, like us, had been trapped in the earthquake. "Oh." I could hear my own disappointment echoed in Jim's one-word response.

"Dan-yell?"

"I am right here, Lukeson."

"You need to keep talking. I heared your voice and join you."

Based on his movements, I did my best to direct him to where I was.

"No, I'm over here." Or, "I can hear you to my left." But in the dark, my guidance essentially amounted to an elaborate game of hot and cold. "Warmer, warmer, hot, boiling hot! Cold."

I worried about him climbing around on the debris. Something could shift underneath him and send a ceiling or wall crashing down. "Be careful, Lukeson!"

"Dan-yell, I hear your voice. I must be close to you, but I can't get there."

His voice sounded like it was right next to me, but I couldn't figure out where he was. "I'm in the elevator. Where are you?"

"I am in the elevator too."

That's when I realized Lukeson was in the elevator *next to me* and trying to climb out of his car so he could join me. The noise I heard was probably him trying to climb up and out and falling back down.

"Can you climb out of your elevator?"

"No, dis is too high."

I suggested several things that Lukeson could try, but the end result was that he wasn't getting out of his elevator. We were like prisoners in adjoining cells. We couldn't see each other or touch each other, but we each felt better knowing the other was there.

"Jim, please add Lukeson to your list."

"I already did."

Lukeson and I talked for a few minutes about what my injuries were, where we were when the quake hit, and whether or not we thought an elevator would be safe during the aftershocks. From what I could understand, Lukeson had been in the elevator the whole time, but he'd only started moving around recently. My best guess was that he'd been unconscious and that when he heard me talking to Jim he woke up and attempted to get out of the elevator. Fortunately, he hadn't sustained any injuries.

After a long pause in our conversation, I started praying again. *Dear Lord, you reminded me that I am yours and I know you still have a purpose for my life. What purpose do you have for me right here in this broken place? How can I be your man in this situation?*

Over the years, I've found that answers to my prayers come in different forms, and sometimes they don't come quickly (at least by my reckoning). Through the early years of our marriage and Christy's depression, I longed to hear God's voice, but often I only experienced silence. During those times, I found myself praying along with the writer of Psalm 13:

> How long, O LORD? Will you forget me forever?
> How long will you hide your face from me?

On those occasions when I did hear God's voice, it most often came quietly into my head. It would come as a thought somehow distinct from my own, as if I were eavesdropping on someone else's mind, and it was always a thought that pointed me in a direction I knew was in line with the Bible.

Here, in my elevator, as much as any time in my life, I longed for God's presence and for quick answers to my prayers. So I was grateful to hear an answer from God so quickly: *"The people trapped near you are hurt, scared, and in need of my love right now. Share my love with them."*

How could I share God's love with others while I was trapped in this elevator?

I could pray with them!

I called out to Jim and the others, "Would you like to pray together?"

Several voices said, "Yes."

"Father," I began, *"we thank you for your love for us, even in hard circumstances."*

I expected I would pray out loud and that the others would just agree quietly or maybe add an Amen when I finished. But as I prayed each phrase, I could hear Jim and the others repeating after me.

My prayer was basically a repeat of the prayers I'd already prayed. I asked God to forgive us for our sins and then asked for comfort, protection, and healing for our wounds. I asked him to be our Savior, and then, *"We ask you for a miracle — please, Lord, rescue us."*

Jim thanked me when I finished. I was comforted to know that God was with me, encouraging me and even using me in this small way. A verse from 2 Chronicles 16 came to mind, "For the eyes of the LORD range throughout the earth to strengthen those whose hearts are fully committed to him."

I finished by adding my own silent prayer to those we'd prayed as a group. *Lord, make my heart completely yours. Thank you for strengthening and supporting me and for sustaining my life. And please, rescue me!*

8

WASHED AWAY

"Dat was good, Dan-yell. Dat was really good."

"Thanks, Lukeson."

As my thoughts shifted to Lukeson, I wondered about his background. *Lord, how can I help Lukeson? He's probably afraid, just like I am, and tonight may be our last night alive. What can I do for him?* I heard a voice in my thoughts, "If I be lifted up, I will draw all men to myself."

Once again, I was grateful that God chose to speak so quickly and so clearly. I understood this message to mean that I should tell Lukeson about Jesus. After all, Lukeson needed a Savior as much as I did.

"Lukeson, are you a follower of Jesus?" I asked.

"I do not understand."

I tried again. "Do you go to church?"

"No, I do not go to the church, Dan-yell."

I took that to mean he wasn't a Christian and didn't know about Jesus. I took a deep breath and prayed about what I should say before I spoke again.

"The reason we prayed to Jesus is because Jesus loves us and can save us. Did you know he is here with us right now?"

"Really?"

"Would you like to know more about Jesus?"

"Yes. Yes, I really would."

I explained that Jesus was God's Son, and even though we were buried in the rubble, Jesus knew where we were and that we were afraid.

"God loves us. He created us to have a relationship, a friendship with him. But sin got in the way and separated us from God."

"Sin? What means *sin*?"

As we talked, I found that every few words I would have to find another way to say what I wanted to communicate so Lukeson could understand. As I tried to choose my words carefully, I found it was helpful to think about how I have explained these things to my boys. I tried to remove all of the religious language and simply and clearly explain God's Word.

"Sins are the wrong things we do, like when we lie, cheat, or do unkind things that God is not pleased with. Do you ever do wrong things?"

"Of course!"

"Sin is the reason we have so many bad things in the world. It's why we have death and killings. Poverty and hunger. Because of sin, the world is broken — and that's why we have earthquakes, hurricanes, and other disasters."

I explained how the Bible tells us that the cost for our sins is eternal suffering in hell — a place apart from God. But God sent Jesus to earth as a man to save us from this punishment. He paid the price for our sins when he died on the cross, and then he showed his power over sin and death when he rose again. He did this to restore our relationship with God. His death is a gift to us. If we accept his gift and are sorry for our sins, we no longer have to pay the price — Jesus has already done it for us.

"The most important rescue of our lives has already happened, Lukeson."

"OK, I understand," Lukeson said. Though he occasionally questioned me when he didn't understand the words I used, it was obvious he was eager to hear what I had to say.

"If you ask Jesus Christ to save you," I continued, "it means that even if you die five minutes from now, you would end up in Jesus' arms and would spend eternity in heaven with him."

"If I died, I would go to heaven and see Jee-sus?"

"Yes, you would. Would you like to accept Jesus Christ as your Savior?"

"Yes, Dan-yell. I really would like dat."

"Then let's pray together."

I led Lukeson in a simple prayer similar to the one I'd prayed with the group.

"Dear Jesus, thank you for dying on the cross to take away my sins."

I could hear Lukeson repeating the words after me.

"Thank you for becoming alive again and that you're with us now. I'm sorry for all the wrong things I do and think. Please forgive me. Help me to live for you, Jesus, for the rest of my life. Please give me a new life and accept me into heaven when I die. I give my life to you, Jesus. Amen."

"Amen."

"That's it, Lukeson; you are a Christian! If you die now, you will go to heaven, and you will meet Jesus."

"Thank you, Dan-yell."

It was his moment of decision, and I could tell he was sincere in his choice to live for God. The moment changed his eternal fate, guaranteeing him everlasting life in heaven. Overwhelming joy welled up inside of me. Even if the rest of the building collapsed and killed us or we died in a few days because we didn't have any food or water, Lukeson's decision meant he would be with Jesus in heaven.

It was also reassuring to know that if by some miracle we were rescued, Lukeson would go on to live life, but now Jesus would be with him. While living for Jesus hadn't made my life easy, Jesus is with us in difficult times and provides purpose for life. I shared this thought with Lukeson.

"If we are rescued and you survive, Jesus will be standing beside you, helping you to live your life. He is your Savior. He will always be with you and a part of your life forever. And he wants you to live your life for him."

I could I hear my new brother in Christ crying, and I knew that Lukeson had understood.

"How does it feel, Lukeson?" I asked.

He answered in a mixture of Creole and English. "Dat feels good, really good. I am so happy — very happy about dat."

I was rejoicing too. I was humbled — and honored — that God would allow me to be a part of this significant moment in Lukeson's life. I knew that God had embraced Lukeson, and I felt as though he had embraced me too, bathing me in his love. I basked in that feeling for some time.

Everyone was quiet. But after a while, I couldn't hold my joy in, so I decided to sing. I started softly: "Great is Thy faithfulness, O God my Father! There is no shadow of turning with Thee." My volume increased, and as I sang the chorus my voice swelled, echoing off the elevator walls. Worshiping felt good, so I continued with a few other hymns and praise songs.

When I finished singing, my thoughts turned to Lukeson again. I wondered what his life would be like if he got out of the elevator alive.

I asked him about his family.

"I have a fiancée. And my moth-er."

Were they injured? Were they even alive?

He had to be thinking the same thing. I thought about how much Lukeson's life had changed. No matter what happened between now and when he died, one day the two of us would meet each other again in heaven.

God had reminded me that I was his man in this situation. This thought comforted me.

According to Scripture, the angels rejoice whenever a person commits his or her life to Jesus. I knew that the angels were having a party in heaven right now because of Lukeson's decision. I liked that picture. I decided to try to lighten the mood in our underground cells.

"Hey Jim," I yelled. "Is the party at your part of the lobby or by the elevators? I'll bring the music if you bring refreshments."

"Let's meet by your elevator. You bring the mu-zak."

Ha! Elevator muzak. Humor fed hope, and hope felt good.

My thoughts drifted to my family. *Was there anything I could do for them while I was in here?*

9

GROUNDHOG DAYS

1994

Pomona, California

We had only been married a few months when we both knew something wasn't right. Less than six months after our wedding, we realized we couldn't fix this by ourselves. Together we went to see a counselor. The counselor's diagnosis of Christy was quick: clinical depression.

The cure was not.

The doctor warned us that it could take months, possibly years, of therapy and adjusting medications before things would be OK. Even then, we'd always have to watch for signs of a relapse.

"I don't understand why this sadness keeps hanging on," I said to her counselor. "Christy's not usually like this. She's the happy person in the room — the first to laugh in any conversation." I wondered how quickly we could get back to our normal lives. "Do you think medication will clear this up soon?"

"I wish it was that easy," the counselor said, sliding her burgundy-rimmed glasses off her nose and laying them on the table next to the pad where she'd been taking notes. "Depression is more complex than you might think." Christy's depression, she explained, might be caused in part by a chemical imbalance in her brain, but her sensitive and empathetic temperament was also a big contributor.

"I don't understand why her temperament would be a problem. I fell in love with Christy in part because of how open she is with her feelings," I said, shifting in my chair.

"Sometimes even our best qualities make us vulnerable to certain challenges. In Christy's case, the same emotional sensitivity that makes her kind and empathetic also makes her ripe to take on and hold on to hurts — her own and others'."

The counselor sighed and looked down at her desk as if she were trying to figure out how to break bad news to me. "Unfortunately, Christy never learned how to deal with these hurts as they came into her life, and she's built up quite a collection. Christy has a lot of work to do, and the medication will help, but if you want her to get well, you're going to have to be involved in the healing process. She can't do it by herself."

The counselor gave us homework. Each night we were to talk about some of Christy's past hurts and disappointments — the ones she stuffed inside and never really dealt with.

This was hard, tedious work for both of us. For Christy, she had to relive some of the most painful wounds from her past. Each time she opened up those closed doors, a torrent of emotions would come flooding out.

I'd have been more patient if we'd been able to follow a predictable pattern or formula — take it out, talk about it, and move on. But it wasn't that simple. At night we'd spend hours talking about incidents from her past, sometimes staying on the same one for weeks or even months. At times it felt like we were having the same conversation day after day. I grew frustrated, bored, and weary of the pace of progress.

———

Living with someone who suffers from clinical depression can be like living through the same unstable day over and over. I was never sure on a given day how Christy would feel. Would she be sad? Unresponsive? Angry? Exhausted? Or would we have a rare day of happiness? There was no point in guessing what the day would bring.

A year and a half into our marriage, Christy rarely smiled anymore. Her once playful eyes seemed devoid of life. I missed my girl — the one who'd dumped water on me as a gag, turned boring days into adventures, and used to laugh at my jokes even when they weren't funny — and most of them weren't.

Though we still loved each other, at this point in our relationship we were no longer best friends. She felt as though I wasn't on her team, and I didn't blame her for feeling that way.

I wasn't the same either. I was more guarded and less open with my feelings than I had once been. I found myself tiptoeing around her feelings, careful not to set off an emotional grenade. I chose my words carefully, positioning them to have the impact on her I desired. Unfortunately, I sometimes crossed the line into manipulation. I'd become more protective of myself and put up walls to keep her pain from spilling all over me. As a result, both of us were mourning the people we *used* to be.

I often got up and dressed for work in the dark to avoid disturbing her. Before I left each morning, I brushed the curls away from her sleeping eyes and kissed her on the cheek. There were so many nights Christy didn't sleep well. She had nightmares more terrifying than any horror movie I've ever seen. Some nights I awoke to her screaming and hitting and kicking me with all of her strength, terrified of visions she had just experienced. On nights like these, she often refused to go back to sleep. I couldn't blame her. Other nights I found her sleepwalking. That always scared me; I was afraid she might hurt herself accidentally. Finally, when her sleep patterns became too unpredictable and the challenges of her career too difficult, Christy had to quit her job.

Around ten o'clock one Monday morning, I called her on the phone. "How ya doing?"

"Fine."

Some days I believed her, but on that morning her voice betrayed her. I pressed a little more. "Are you sure?"

"You know how I'm doing." That was always code for "not well."

I reminded her that I was praying for her. Sometimes I prayed for her over the phone. Today, though, I thought I'd try to remind her of happier times. "Remember that weekend we went to the beach? Let's do that again soon. That was fun."

"Yeah."

"Maybe Sunday?"

"Maybe."

Sometimes I'd tell her a joke or talk about something funny that happened at work, but often there was no response. I would do anything I could to lighten her mood, but when it didn't happen, I felt as if I had failed. *If I were funnier, would it make a difference? Could I make her smile?*

"Just a couple more hours, Sweet, and I'll be home."

I wrapped things up and left by six. During the transition from work to home, I prepared myself to be supportive. *Be gentle. Don't come on too strong. Make sure she can hear love in your voice.*

While talking to myself, I could feel physical changes taking place in my body. My gut wrenched, my face tightened, and I started to breathe faster. *If she's mad, don't react; just try to listen.* As I tensed up, it felt as though I was building — brick by brick — the emotional walls that separated us.

We felt little distinction between days. It seemed like one long day, or perhaps the same day repeated for years. In an effort to break the monotony, each night I'd experiment with things we had talked about in counseling; I'd paint a hopeful picture of the future, remind her of good times in the past, or pray with her — but the results rarely changed.

When I came into the apartment, Christy stood at the stove making dinner. I could tell she was feeling especially down. I walked over and hugged her. Before I could think of something encouraging to say, she spoke. "There is nothing good in my life. Nothing positive. Everything in my life is sad."

I knew this was the depression talking. While I wanted to try to change her perspective by reminding her of all the good things in our lives, I stopped myself. I knew from experience that trying to convince her of something she didn't believe would usually result in an argument. Instead, I was learning through counseling to respond in ways that acknowledged what she was feeling and gave room for her emotions. Listening and processing through these feelings without offering quick solutions went against my natural fix-it nature that tended to look for easy answers.

"Oh, honey, I'm sorry you're feeling so sad. It must be so hard to see things that way." I took a step back so I could look into her eyes.

I did my best to point out some of the blessings in her life without negating her experiences and perceptions. But often I got it wrong. Sometimes my impatience got the best of me, and I reacted in frustration. Sometimes my response was so contrived that whatever I said smacked of insincerity. I was like the photographer who says, "Tilt your head to the left, stick your chin out, look to the right, and move your ears back. Now smile, and act natural."

As I drained the pot of spaghetti, I reminded myself that we did have some enjoyable times. Some nights I'd pick up dinner on my way home, and we'd watch a movie together or play cards and enjoy a pleasant evening. But it was hard for Christy to remember her moments of happiness. Two weeks later, she'd already forgotten those happy times.

We piled our plates with spaghetti and sauce and sat in our usual chairs. As I watched her pick at her food, I knew she was spending too much time alone in the dark apartment while I was at work. She needed to experience life and to feel the sunlight on her skin. And I wanted to see her smile.

"What do you think about going to the zoo on Saturday? They have a new baby giraffe. We should go see what she's like."

She stared at her plate. I watched as she took a forkful of spaghetti, twirled it three times, and raised it to her mouth. She chewed slowly before she responded. "Maybe."

I reminded her of the zoo idea throughout the week to try to give her something to look forward to. On Wednesday, I asked her if she was looking forward to going.

Her response was noncommittal. "I'm not sure I'm up to it."

On Friday, I was still hopeful. "I stopped at the store on the way home from work and picked up some bread, deli meat, and apples so we can pack lunches for the zoo tomorrow."

"I'm not sure I want to go. I don't think I have the energy for it."

I recalled so many previous visits to the zoo and her delight in discovering new things about the animals and then educating me about them. Christy loved to learn, and as a teacher she had loved to share her knowledge with others. To see her lack of enthusiasm now broke my heart, but it didn't prevent me from prodding her.

Saturday morning, I got up around eight and gently woke her.

"Please, I'm so tired — can I just sleep a little longer?"

I got dressed and packed our lunches. Around ten, I checked on her again.

"Can't we just stay here today?"

Too many times in the past, I'd agreed. But I wanted her to have a fun, memorable day.

"I know you're tired, Christy, but the sun is shining outside. Let's go enjoy it."

I was glad to see her push back the covers and slowly get out of bed.

In the car, she sat listlessly looking out the window at the traffic. She barely spoke a word, so I chatted the whole way there. I talked about the animals we'd see, our favorite picnic spot for lunch, and whether or not we could make it in time to see the hippos being fed.

The meerkat exhibit always made us laugh, so we headed there first. I couldn't help but be amused by their silly facial expressions as they stood on their hind legs, looking out from under their dark, furry eyebrows. One pup was begging for food from his mother, and I pointed it out to Christy, laughing harder than necessary at the pup's antics. But she didn't react. I realized I was overdoing it. *You can't make her have a good time by contriving the situation.* I felt stupid for even trying.

The difference between this trip and our previous trips was obvious to both of us. In the past, she never grew tired of the zoo. An interesting detail about an exhibit would grab her attention, and she would want to tell me about it. We would walk around holding hands and laughing at inside jokes. But on this trip, nothing seemed to catch her interest. As we walked through the exhibits, I thought about how long it had been since I'd seen her laugh.

I didn't plan on stopping at the gazelle exhibit, but Christy saw something. She turned to me and said, "Gazelles jump higher than a human head — can you imagine?"

I didn't catch all of what she was saying. I only heard a few words because I was focused on her slight smile as she said it. My heart turned somersaults. I nodded in agreement with whatever she'd just said, and I laughed out loud — because she *smiled* when she said it. I'd just seen a glimpse of my girl, and it felt so good.

We made our way to the picnic area and pulled out our lunches. We had a pleasant conversation, and Christy smiled and even chuckled a time or two. I enjoyed this moment of relative normalcy.

A few days later, when I called from work, I reminded her of our day at the zoo. "That was fun, wasn't it? It was great to get out of the house and go somewhere together."

"It's hard for me to remember."

What I had hoped would be a fun, memorable experience was already blending into the gray monotony of our days.

———

I often felt myself mourning the loss of the relationship we once had but which no longer existed. I wanted to be angry with God, but the truth was that I needed him so much I couldn't. Instead, I'd get angry with myself. *If only I were more capable, more patient, or more loving.*

I begged God to heal her. I prayed for the synapses and the neurons in her head. I prayed for myself — for supernatural wisdom, for patience, and for protection against unwarranted negativity. Perhaps my most common prayer was: *God, help me do better today than I did yesterday.*

Yet as Christy's suffering increased, I sometimes felt like God was not listening to my desperate prayers for her healing, and I went through periods where God felt very distant. *Why was he not intervening?*

———

A few weeks after the zoo trip, Christy was not feeling well and asked me to put a movie into the VCR before I left for work. When I came home, she was still watching the same movie. "What happened? Why didn't you watch it when I started it for you this morning?"

"I did."

"You're watching it again now?"

"Yes."

"How many times have you watched this movie today?"

"Five."

The movie was *Groundhog Day*. It was the story of weatherman Phil Connors, played by Bill Murray, who was forced to relive the same day — over and over again. Christy had chosen a movie about repetition, and then she watched it repeatedly.

This was the life we were living, and I now had a term for the monotonous days. They were our *Groundhog Days*.

10

SAYING GOOD-BYE

Tuesday Night

Hotel Montana, Port-au-Prince

Darkness can do funny things to your mind. During, and immediately after the quake, the inability to see terrified me — I thought I'd gone blind. After I turned on my camera and saw the light, I realized how powerful and oppressive the blackness was. The lack of light directly affected my safety — I had to feel for everything and I wasn't always sure what I was touching. As I groped through my surroundings, I knew I was risking another injury.

My world had suddenly gotten very small, not only because of the elevator's size, but because I found myself taking refuge in my thoughts. But my hearing was so much more acute that I was often startled by new sounds. Something as simple as Lukeson shifting in his elevator sent adrenaline pulsing through my veins. My remaining senses were on high alert, twitching at each foreign sensation. I could understand how people went mad in the dark.

However, I also found comfort in what were fast becoming familiar sounds: the trickle of debris in distant parts of the building, Lukeson's lilting Haitian accent, and Jim's deep voice and the muted conversations of those who were with him. These things reminded me that I was still alive. These sounds calmed my fears in this dark and confusing environment.

I felt fortunate that I had been on walkabouts in college where I spent two days and a night by myself in the wilderness near Yosemite, a unique opportunity for undistracted alone time with God. Night in the wilderness was challenging, and during that night alone, my goals were to get a little sleep, keep warm, and hang on until the morning. In the outdoors, morning represented sunlight, color, and warm relief from the evening chill. But here in my urban cave, light took on new meaning. If I ever saw daylight again, it would mean rescue — and reunion with my family.

It was late; I checked my phone for the time — a few minutes before midnight. I knew that rescuers were more likely to show up in the morning when they could see what they were doing. So I asked God to help me hold on until morning. I tried to get as comfortable as possible while I waited for the dawn I wouldn't be able to see from my shelter.

I tried lying on my back, bending my knees slightly and putting my feet up against the wall. But that meant my back was pressed against even more rocks, so I didn't stay in that position for long. It didn't take long for me to realize that no matter what I did, it wasn't going to be a comfortable night.

"Dan, how are you and your Haitian friend doing?"

I appreciated that Jim would periodically check on us. How long had it been since I last talked to Lukeson?

"How are you, Lukeson?"

"I fine, Dan-yell."

Though Lukeson was in the elevator to my left as I looked toward the lobby, and though Jim could hear me best when I directed my voice to the left, Lukeson and Jim couldn't seem to hear each other well. "We're all OK over here. How are you guys?" Whenever I yelled to Jim, I always felt like I was talking past Lukeson.

"We're good too."

Occasionally, I could hear Jim talking to Sarla, the woman who was near their group but not trapped with them. She had some mobility, and they were trying to see if she could safely move to an area where she might be able to signal an outsider. But she was as much in the dark as the rest of us. I didn't think there was much hope of her making contact during the night.

As the night wore on, I spent more time thinking about my family. I knew that by now, Christy would have heard about the earthquake. I tried to imagine what happened when she heard. How was she holding up? And how scared were the boys? *Dear Father, is there anything I can do for them from here? How can I be your man for my family while I am at the bottom of a collapsed building two thousand miles away from home?* If I could just have one more conversation with Christy and the boys.

My journal!

I always carried a moleskin journal in my pants pocket. To me it was more than just a journal; it was my catchall for details during my day — to-do lists, random phone numbers, shopping lists. I patted the outside of my pants pocket; it was still there along with a couple of pens. I reached in and pulled them out.

I was thankful for the opportunity to leave them a few last words before I died, but it also broke my heart to know I had to leave good-bye *notes* because I might never speak to them again. There was so much left unsaid, especially with Christy.

I used the camera to see what I was doing. I flashed the auto-focus light to get a glimpse of a page. After the light flashed, I tried to remember what I'd just seen. I had to go through several pages of the journal to find a blank one. When I did, I placed my thumb in position so I knew where to start writing. I put the camera down and then aligned the pen with my thumb. Doing this, I could scratch out a few lines at a time.

I wrote:

If found, please give to my wife, Christina.
I love you.

After two or three lines, I stopped, picked up the camera, and pressed the autofocus button to find a blank spot where I could reposition my thumb. Then I'd put the camera down, pick up the pen, and try to remember what I'd just seen so I didn't write over my own words. It was tedious work.

I have never stopped loving you or even slowed down.

I wanted the very first note I wrote to be about my love for her. I was pretty sure that lately she hadn't felt much love and affection from me. It made me sad to think that although we had been through so much together, somehow we had let busy schedules, bad habits, and poor prioritization of our time push us apart.

How did I let things get so out of control? I wished I had gotten this right with her when we were face-to-face. Instead of telling her how much I loved her in person and showing her in our day-to-day lives, I was writing it in a poorly scrawled note. But the note was still a blessing. If I was going to die and leave her with a seemingly impossible life, at least I could let her know that my love for her was as deep and real as it had ever been.

I started thinking about my boys. At six and three years old, I was afraid they wouldn't remember many of our conversations and the guidance I'd provided them up until now. It pained me to think my influence on their lives might be limited by time.

I love Josh and Nathan, the joy and pride of my life.

Boys hold on to the things their fathers say. Whether it's a compliment, a favorite quote, a rebuke, or a swearword, boys pick up those words when they're young and carry them for the rest of their lives. *What could I say that would make some difference in their lives?* I knew whatever I wrote, Christy would display it as a keepsake for them. It would be one of their last memories of their dad, and I wanted to make it count.

Josh, choose the right path every day. If you stumble, get back on the right path. With your kindness and love for God, you can be a great leader of men. Don't just live. Change the world!

As a family, we had been talking about character, and we'd had several conversations about getting on the right path — God's path —

and staying there. I wanted Josh to know that I remembered those conversations, and I wanted him to remember them too. I'd already seen his character growing — even at such a young age. His character and his relationship with God were the most important things he had. They would shape the choices he made and establish his trajectory in this life and into eternity.

Recently, I'd begun to notice how Josh really seemed to need my approval, and I tried to give it to him, freely and often. With each word of praise, his face lit up — he had a smile just like his mother's. I wanted him to know I thought he was up to the challenges that life would bring his way.

My sons were "all boy," and on Sunday mornings we let the testosterone loose. We attended church on Saturday nights so we could let Christy sleep in on Sunday mornings. It was the one time a week I got to spend time alone with the boys. Some mornings we'd take advantage of Colorado's outdoor activities, like hiking or riding bikes. On days I was moving a little slower, we watched testosterone TV. At six, Josh was really into building his own creations with Legos, so he loved shows like "Prototype This," in which crack teams of scientists and engineers created wacky inventions.

We all enjoyed watching Bear Grylls demonstrate his survival skills in harsh wilderness environments. Josh and I had to turn away when Bear ate gross things on his show *Man vs. Wild*, but Nathan loved it. Watching television with the boys on Sunday mornings may not have been the best parenting ever, but I liked to think the boys learned something about creative problem solving and how to use available resources.

Nathan was into physical play and was usually the first to suggest wrestling or lightsaber fights. And he always wanted to do things his big brother did. I hadn't yet figured out whether his need for routines and structure were because of his age or just built into his personality. He liked strict adherence to his bedtime routine, and he seldom varied the last words he said to us each night after we tucked him in: "Good night, I love you. Jesus is with you. See you in the morning. In the morning let's play Star Wars: The Clone Wars."

Nathan, I'm sorry I wasn't there to get to know you better, but I already love your laugh and smile. I love wrestling with you.

Thinking about the boys' future, I realized how natural it would be for them to be mad at God as they got older. I also knew this might be Christy's response too. "How could you, God?" was a natural question in a situation like this. I wanted them to ask their questions honestly and openly, without turning away from God. I knew God was big enough to handle our questions, and he wasn't afraid of our anger. I hoped they could eventually move past the anger to trust in God's goodness, despite this tragedy.

I was in a big accident (earthquake). Don't be upset at God. He always provides for his children, even in hard times. I'm still praying that God will get me out. He may not, but he will always take care of you.

I wrote the words for the boys, but also for Christy. And there was more I needed to say to her. Once again, I flicked on the auto-focus, but when I went to set the camera down, I dropped my pen. I groped around on the floor, but I couldn't locate it among the chunks of concrete and debris. Fortunately, I always carried multiple pens and was able to reach into my pocket for another one.

Don't give up, Christy, no matter how hard. God will make a way.

I didn't want to smear the journal with my tears. I knew that since I was writing in the dark, it would already be difficult to decipher, but I couldn't stop the flood of emotions. Frequently, I stopped writing and cried. I was saying good-bye to *my family*. Once the torrent of tears passed, I got back to writing. I turned over onto my back and lifted the journal above me to avoid dripping more tears onto the pages.

Rely on the love of friends and get counseling.

I hoped my words to Christy would speak to her heart and fend off any downward spiral toward depression. I hoped she would take my advice as much as possible.

Please turn to God. He is real. His promises are real.

I knew that in a crisis like this, Christy would be attacked by doubts and negative thoughts that could draw her away from God. I hoped my voice would join other voices in her life encouraging her to hold on to the faith in Jesus that we shared.

It was late. I was tired, and I didn't feel like I had a lot of strength left. I wanted to conserve my camera battery, because I didn't know when I might need it again. So I wrote short messages. I did my best to comfort Christy, but the whole thing felt so inadequate. This was not the way I would have planned to say good-bye. But if this was all I had and God had given me this last opportunity to communicate with my family, then I was going to do everything I could.

My biggest regrets are not spending more time discipling with God and not doing more to keep my love life more on fire with you. I really did enjoy all of our years together, Christy! Even the bitter-sweet or just-making-it years.

Before I'd left, Christy had asked me to leave detailed information about our financial accounts — which bills were due when and to whom. But I had neglected to do it. I turned to a new blank page and did my best to make it up to her. I wrote up lists of practical things, like how to access our online banking information, passwords for my e-mail accounts, and details of how to access our assets and pay bills. I told her how to sell our online business and suggested a minimum price and the names of a couple of potential buyers, as well as friends from work who could help her pull it all together. I explained how I made money in the side businesses that I ran and from whom she should collect payments. These were all things I had handled; unfortunately, I'd never shared the information with Christy.

I also wrote my last will and testament. I wasn't sure if it would hold up in court, but I did my best in case it helped.

It was important to me to make sure I did everything I could to make life easier for her. I was sad that chronicling these practical details took three times as much space and time as the personalized notes. But I considered these lists love letters too — just ones I wished I had written a long time ago.

I thought about David's family and wondered what their situation was. I realized I needed to leave information for rescuers and his family in case they read my journal. So I wrote:

I think my friend David may be unconscious or dead. I'm praying for him and his family.

My pen stopped working.
And I freaked out.

11

FATAL MISTAKE

Lying on my back and writing upside down had caused the ink to run dry. I sat up, shook the pen, and tried drawing little circles in the margins to get the flow back. I even tried sucking the ink capsule to get it started, but nothing I did could get the pen to work again.

How dumb could I be? I had dropped and lost a pen earlier, and now I'd been foolish enough to use the second one upside down. I reached into my pocket, hoping to find another one. The only thing that remained was a Sharpie. I tried to use it to write, but it had a fat tip, and the ink bled through the pages of my journal so I could only write short sentences on one side of a page. I flashed the camera and looked for pages that were blank on both sides.

There was more I wanted to say. I didn't want to leave my family with the image that I had died alone and in pain when the truth was that I felt God with me the whole time.

I'm only in a little pain. I'm calm, talking with God.

It surprised me how much I felt God's presence in this dark hole and how I heard answers to some of my prayers so quickly. When tragedy strikes, we often feel neglected by God and wonder if he's even out there. I hoped my experience of his presence would encourage Christy and the boys.

God is very real. He is with me now.

Next, I thought of my mom and four sisters and wondered how they were handling the news that I was missing. I missed them. I was sad that we were so spread out across the country. I wrote messages of love to them and told them I hoped we would be reunited in heaven. My sister Mimmy was the organizer in the family and one of the best family members to lean on in a crisis. I asked her to help Christy with the funeral arrangements.

I put the cap back on the Sharpie. I was thankful that I had the opportunity to leave them notes, but it felt like such a pathetic way to say good-bye to the people I loved most.

———

Christy and I were a team. After homeschooling and shuttling our kids to various activities, she was often worn out by the end of the day. In the evenings, she relied on me to help get the boys to bed, join in on the household chores, and be available to discuss and process experiences from her day. She didn't like it when I went away on business trips; she didn't sleep well. Our boys are well behaved but have the high energy levels common to young boys. By the time I returned home from a trip, she was usually stretched pretty thin. *What will it be like for her if I never return?*

The boys counted on me to shake things up with them. Much of their time with Christy was spent on structured homeschooling or school-related activities. When I spent time with the boys, it was all spontaneity and boy-play. We'd get out the lightsabers and alien ships. We played David and Goliath and did a lot of outdoor activities. *Where would they find an outlet for these kinds of activities?* The boys were so young, and so much of their future was unknown. What would their personalities be like? Would they hang out with the wrong crowd? Would they be like some of my friends who gave up on God when they got older?

That was my worst fear.

I pictured the boys without a dad. I worried that they would blame God, and I feared how that might undermine their faith.

———

Lying on my right side was the most comfortable, but it hurt when my knees touched. While moving things around, I found a stone with a flat top that was about the size of my shoe. I stacked it on top of another stone and it became my rock pillow. I felt around the floor until I found another flat rock, approximately the size of a notebook, and two inches thick. I put it between my knees, raising my injured leg up a bit to slightly reduce my pain. I closed my eyes; not that it mattered because the view didn't change.

I licked dust from my dry lips and thought about how thirsty I was. I remembered seeing an episode of *Man vs. Wild* with the boys. The host of the show — wilderness adventurer and survival expert Bear Grylls — said it was possible to die of dehydration in three days. *Wow. Just three days?*

From my experience working with international relief organizations, I knew that many logistical delays slowed the delivery of rescue equipment and personnel to a disaster, especially in poverty-ridden countries like Haiti. If rescuers came from the United States, it might take them three days just to transport themselves and their gear to Haiti.

I tried not to think about it. I was as comfortable as I could get. I decided I needed to get some sleep, to rest up for whatever would come next. I closed my eyes and tried to relax. The symptoms of shock had passed, and I was no longer worried about not waking up.

But as I quietly lay there, I felt it. There was a pressure in my bladder.

I have to urinate.

Once I had the thought, there was no way I could to go to sleep until I'd done something about it. I hadn't gone to the bathroom since the morning and hadn't felt the urge before. But now that I was aware I had to go, I had to go quickly.

Should I just go in my pants?

No. I wasn't going to do that.

I used the handrail bar in the back of the elevator to hoist myself up. Once I was standing, I put my weight on my right leg.

How ironic. I need water, and now water will be flowing from my body. *If only there was a way to hold on to it.*

I didn't want the wetness or the smell inside my elevator car, but I didn't want to step outside of the elevator until I was sure it was safe. I quickly lifted my camera toward the lobby and took a picture so that I could examine the walls before I stepped out. I took a glance at the picture. The walls seemed stable enough for me to take care of business. If another aftershock came, I could dive back into the elevator.

As I unzipped my pants, I remembered the details of that *Man vs. Wild* episode. Bear said if you were ever in a situation where you faced dehydration, drinking urine could help extend the time frame. Then he demonstrated by drinking his.

It was just one of many episodes that made Josh and me squeamish. Bear would eat bugs or raw meat fresh off a carcass. We'd turn our heads and say, "Yuck! That's gross." While watching those kinds of episodes, we had wondered if all of that was really necessary. "Why doesn't he at least cook the meat first?" Josh had asked.

"I guess when you're in a situation like that, you do whatever it takes to survive."

At the time, I never would have guessed I'd be in such a situation one day. Here, I understood Bear's actions much better. In desperate times you do what you have to do to prolong your life. Without question I would eat raw meat, chew on bugs, or drink my own urine. No second thoughts about it.

Bear had taken off his shirt and urinated into it, then squeezed it into his mouth. He made a face and said, "Oh, that's really bad."

Do I really want to do this? Without hesitation, I knew I did. I have survived a major earthquake. I'm not going to let squeamishness about drinking my urine stop me from getting back to my family.

I'd already used my outer shirt to wrap my leg, so my black T-shirt was all I had left. I took it off and stepped one foot outside of the elevator, so I could aim outside of the shaft. I cupped the shirt in front of me and urinated directly into it. When I was finished, I lifted it above my lips and let it trickle in, then squeezed it so I would get every drop. The warm liquid had a salty and very unpleasant taste. After I got a mouthful, I quickly swallowed it.

Though the experience was very distasteful, having moisture in my mouth and liquid running down my throat did more to relieve the extreme dryness and thirst than I had expected. But more importantly, it gave me confidence that I was doing something tangible to help my chances of survival, and that fact lifted my spirits and made me feel like I had at least a little bit of control over my circumstances.

Bear had hung his shirt on a tree branch to dry. I knew it would take mine longer to dry here, underground. I hung the shirt on the handrail in the elevator, spreading it out so the maximum surface area would be exposed to the air.

I lay back down on the spot that had previously measured "tolerable" on my comfort meter. But this time I was shirtless, and the rocks ruthlessly stabbed me in the back and clung to my side. The concrete was cool. Almost immediately, I started shivering. Still, I was glad to have Haiti's tropical heat rather than Colorado's frigid winter nights.

But I couldn't sleep because of my shivering. Soon my teeth were chattering. I thought about adventure and survival stories I'd read and remembered survivors who described the fatal mistakes that cost the lives of others on their expedition. It was a different mistake in each situation, but the point was made that all it took to separate the survivors from the deceased was one fatal mistake.

I hugged myself and curled into a ball trying to stay warm. Maintaining a normal body temperature was a critical factor in survival situations. Cold was a dangerous killer. *Would I develop hypothermia? Was soaking my shirt a fatal mistake?* I hadn't made a mistake so far, but I started to think this might be my first.

I realized it could also be my last.

12

CALLS

1996

Monrovia, California

One thing that broke up the monotony of those endless repeating *Groundhog Days* was Christy's phone calls to me while I was at work. I didn't know when to expect them or what she would say.

Christy saw the world through the distorted lenses of her depression glasses. As her self-esteem melted away, she imagined or exaggerated slights from others. She would call me at work to tell me how someone had wronged her.

"You'll never believe the way that clerk looked at me," she'd say, crying.

Instead of sympathizing, I rushed to tell her how wrong she was. "Now, Christy, I'm sure you're reading too much into it." I quickly learned how futile and insensitive that approach was.

Though concentrating at work was more difficult with the interruptions, I was glad to hear her voice and know how she was doing. She fought tenaciously against the depression, learning to identify unhealthy thoughts and working to replace them with positive ones. To help with this, she carried around a notebook of Bible verses, song lyrics, and other reminders of the beauty found in the world around her. But for a "fixer" like me, it never felt like enough.

By our third year of marriage, I found myself impatient, wishing that things would move along at a faster pace. Christy sensed my frustrations, and it only made things harder between us.

———

The worst phone call I ever received came on a Thursday. I was working on a project in my office, and my mind was elsewhere as I answered the phone. "This is Dan."

There was a pause before I heard the response. It was Christy, and I knew there was a problem. "I won't be here when you get home." My heart dropped into my stomach.

"What do you mean?"

"I really don't want to do life anymore. I'm done."

I wondered if this was a real threat or a cry for help. She knew my mother had killed herself and that I would take the threat very seriously. Either way, I had to respond quickly. "Christy, I need to know how serious you are about this."

Things had been getting worse for weeks. She hadn't been sleeping much, and she was more withdrawn. I pressed the receiver to my ear, but I couldn't hear any crying. She sounded like she was drained of all life. Her voice was weak and devoid of emotion, almost monotone.

I was terrified. Suicide is always a threat to take very seriously. *Lord, is this it? Please don't let this happen!*

"Where are you? Do you have a plan?" I could feel the panic rising in my throat.

"Yes, I'm going to do it in the bathtub. I don't want to leave too much of a mess. I just didn't want you to be surprised when you got home."

My vision narrowed. Blackness was closing in on me. *Please help me, Lord.*

"Christy, listen to me." I found a desperate strength from deep inside of me. "I'm coming home *now*! I'll be home in three minutes. Can you stop and hold on until I get there? Then we can talk about how you're feeling and why it hurts so much."

"You're coming home now? I don't know ..."

"I need you to promise me you will be safe, or you know I'll have to call 911. Should I call 911?"

There was a pause. "No."

"Will you hold on until I get there?"

"Yes. If I can …"

"I know you can do this, Christy. I need you to promise to be safe until I get home."

Her response was weak, but sincere. "OK, I promise."

I hung up the phone and reached for my keys, knocking a plant off my desk and spilling dirt all over the floor. But I didn't care, I'd clean it up tomorrow — or whenever I came back. *If* I came back.

My mind was spinning, and I felt dizzy as I raced down the hall. I ran into my boss on the stairs. "I can't talk now. I'll explain later. I've got to get home; there's an emergency."

I knew I couldn't explain to my boss what was happening. At that time, Christy's depression was still a dark secret that she and I kept well hidden. She felt so much embarrassment and shame about it that she didn't want anyone to know. We hadn't even told our families the full depth of our struggle.

Dear God, please don't let anything happen. Just keep her safe until I get there.

I honestly didn't know what I would find when I got to the apartment. I wondered if I should have called 911, but now that we were living closer to my office, I knew I would get there before the paramedics would anyway.

When I got to our apartment, I pulled into the parking space and ran for the stairs. The door was locked. My heart was already beating fast, but now it strained to its limit as I fumbled for my key and put it in the lock. I threw open the door. As I passed the bathroom, I saw that the light was on and there was water in the tub, but no Christy. A knife lay on the edge of the tub, but the blade was clean. I took several deep breaths before slowly walking to our bedroom.

As I opened the door, I tried to let go of my fear. *Be sensitive. Be gentle. Now, of all times, love her unconditionally.*

She was in bed with the covers pulled over her head. I took off my shoes and gently climbed in beside her.

"How are you feeling?"

"It hurts so much."

"Tell me what it feels like."

"I feel like I am in a hole. It is deep and dark, and I'm suffocating. It's terrifying. I keep clawing to get just a handful of something so I can pull myself up, but whatever I grab just crumbles in my hand."

"Oh, honey." I shifted so I could stretch my arm underneath her and pull her close to me. "I am so sorry; I am so very sorry."

"I was going to do it. I was really going to do it, Dan."

We had spent hours in counseling talking about her thoughts of hurting herself, but we also had an agreement that she would call me or 911 if she ever really thought she would go through with it. If she broke that promise, she knew what the consequences could be: she would have to be hospitalized.

"What stopped you?"

"I didn't want to hurt you. You deserve better than this."

"Thank you for calling me." I looked into her face. Her eyes were dull and vacant. "I can't imagine how hard it was for you to call me, but I'm so glad you did." I stroked her cheek and kissed her forehead.

She stared into my eyes as if she were trying to read something inside of me.

"I'm not getting better."

I didn't flinch or blink. I kept my eyes locked with hers and answered with as much hope as I could convincingly muster. "We're going to get through this. It will get better. We just have to keep going forward — one step at a time."

"Is this what our life is going to be like forever?"

"No, it's not. I know God has better things ahead for us."

"Like what? Every time I hope for something, it goes away."

I needed to give her hope. I needed to paint a picture of our future that was very different from where we were now — a future I wasn't confident we'd ever see.

"Hey, we're going to get through this, and we're going to have kids one day. You are going to be such an amazing mom. I can already see you teaching them. On weekends, we'll take them on the best field trips any child has experienced. We'll explore museums and farms and coral reefs. We'll take them camping and hiking — "

"The way I am now, that could never happen."

She argued with me because she couldn't see past the hurt. I couldn't completely see it either, but I didn't let that stop me. "I believe it will happen, Sweet. You're going to get better. Then our kids will get older, and one day we'll have grandkids. We'll have them over to the house and play games. We'll be so old and so in love we won't even mind turning up each other's hearing aids and washing each other's dentures."

She stopped arguing and let me tell her stories about our future. It had been days since she'd slept for more than a couple of hours at a time, and I could tell that exhaustion was catching up with her. "I'll rub your back to help you fall asleep."

I focused on making slow patterns on her back with my fingertips. I prayed out loud for Christy to hear, and I prayed silent desperate prayers she couldn't hear. I kept talking, hoping the sound of my voice would transport her to a brighter future. Even if that future was tomorrow morning, and even if *brighter* meant she felt a little less hopeless.

As I talked, she slowly closed her eyes. I watched as the frown lines on her face eased slightly. Eventually sheer exhaustion won. I held her in my arms until she dozed off, thanking God for saving her life. By the time sleep came, the darkness of night had overtaken the apartment.

Gingerly, I scooted to the side of the bed and put one foot and then the other on the floor until I could quietly creep out of bed. I stopped in the doorway of our bedroom and watched Christy sleep. For the first time in days, she was free from the searing pain of her tortured mind.

I went to the bathroom, grabbed the knife, and turned off the light. I hid it in an unused drawer in the kitchen before I climbed back into bed.

Though I was next to my wife, I felt like I was all alone in the dark. I longed for God to comfort me, to reassure me of a brighter future just as I had comforted and reassured Christy.

Dear Father, I want kids. Grandkids. I want to grow old with Christy and even deeper in love. I want everything I described to her. But it doesn't seem like it's going to happen. Is this what our life is going to be like? Will it always be day after day of darkness? If this is what your will is for us, if it is my job to be here for her through this struggle, I accept that. I will do it faithfully and lovingly for as long as you desire, because she is worth it. But please, I beg of you, give us more. She deserves better than this from life. Bring us out of this dark valley and into green fields on the other side.

Buried underneath the covers, I didn't hear God speak, and there was no peace or comfort that washed over me. Instead, fatigue overtook my body.

13

GOD IS GOOD?

Wednesday Morning

Hotel Montana, Port-au-Prince

I spent the next hour shivering. Every few minutes, I reached up to touch my T-shirt, knowing it still wouldn't be dry. *How long can I continue to be this cold without harming my health?* When I couldn't stand it any longer, I reached up, squeezed out the excess liquid, and put the shirt back on. It was no longer wet, just damp, and it was better to be in the T-shirt than not.

It was still too early for the sun to have risen. I guessed it was sometime between three and four in the morning — ten or so hours after the earthquake.

I tried to compare the damage I'd witnessed as a teenager during a California earthquake to what might have happened in Haiti. During the Whittier quake in 1987, I watched as dinner plates shook and fell off shelves. The floor swayed, and some walls developed minor cracks.

I could only imagine the damage this quake had done to Port-au-Prince, as it was obviously much worse than anything I'd experienced in California.

The few trained rescuers in a poverty-ridden country like Haiti would be undertrained and underequipped. In addition, if communications were down and roads were damaged, rescuers from outside

95

Haiti would have a hard time getting in. My best guess, based on my experience with relief organizations, was that rescue teams coming from the United States and other countries wouldn't arrive until the weekend. *That's at least seventy-two more hours! Can I make it that long?*

I thought of David and how he had only been two or three feet away from me when the earthquake struck. I had been hoping he was unconscious, but surely if he were still alive, he would have regained consciousness by now and made himself known by speaking or tapping. David was resourceful. As a filmmaker on a budget, he had to be. If he tried to get my attention, I was sure I or one of the survivors near me would have heard him by now. I resigned myself to the thought that if he hadn't gotten our attention yet, he wasn't able to.

I recalled the picture I'd taken of the lobby a while earlier. Perhaps by studying it, I could get a better idea of what happened. I picked up my dust-covered camera and turned it on. My bloody fingerprints were all over the screen, making it hard to see anything. I moved the dial to the review mode and pressed the button to bring up the last image. The screen was small, so I squinted to make out the details. Most of the elements in the picture were white and gray. I could see the cracked support beam and the fallen ceiling. There was a reddish-brown rectangular object jutting out from underneath the fallen concrete ceiling.

What is that?

At first, I couldn't make sense of what I was seeing. Then my chest tightened and heat spread from my neck to my face as it occurred to me that the rusty, red color was likely blood. What would be coming out from under the concrete slab and covered in blood?

The horror hit me as I realized what I was looking at. *That's David's leg!*

I broke into tears. I'd already assumed David had died immediately, but this was the confirmation I had hoped I'd never get. *Why, God, why?*

I pounded my fist on the floor, and the pain shot through my arm. Seeing the picture fit exactly with what I recalled in my mind.

David had been next to me when the quake struck. And in one horrible moment, he was gone.

I remembered diving toward the stairs, and I'd always pictured David lunging in the same direction. Apparently, we'd been separated just long enough for the ceiling to miss me and hit him.

I felt sick to my stomach. I wanted to throw up. I fought the urge, knowing that it wouldn't help anything. I thought of the short time David and I had spent together. He was so accomplished and skilled as a filmmaker, and his love for his family was so evident.

I thought about his family. My tears flowed as I wondered how they would handle this loss. I considered the challenges they would face. *God, how could this ever be a good thing for them?*

I knew David was in heaven, that things were better for him now than ever before. But what about his family? Romans 8:28 reads, "And we know that in all things God works for the good of those who love him, who have been called according to his purpose." How in the world could God work this out for the good?

Father, why did you allow this to happen? I know my mind and my perspectives are so limited, but help me understand how David's death could result in anything but pain. It looks like I might die here too. How could leaving a mother without a father for her children ever be part of your good plan?

Please give me comfort in this crisis, and please give my family peace. I know they're worried and trying to figure out what to do. Please be with Christy. I know she could crumble right now, but I also know she can be a mother bear and fight for her family. Please give her the strength to fight. And protect my boys from the images and messages that are too scary for them to understand.

If I don't make it out of here alive, Jesus, please embrace my boys. Be their dad and miraculously fill the hole I've left in our family. And be a husband and provider to Christy.

I had significant issues with my own father when I was in junior high. At a particularly hard time, I remember asking God to be my true father. From that moment on, I felt as if God fulfilled the role of the father I needed, making up for many of my earthly dad's failings. I prayed that my sons would have a similar experience.

But even as I prayed, I kept coming back to visions of things not going well for Christy and the boys, and I felt the tension in me increasing.

God, I don't understand why you would bring David and me here to die. Why did you allow this to happen? Are Ephraim and Johnnie dead also? Missoul and her daughters? How many thousands of Haitians have died in this tragedy? I don't understand how you can bring anything good out of this situation. Please help me understand.

During my prayers, I had thrown some tough questions at God. I didn't expect a quick answer, nor did I receive one. I also didn't experience any peace. It didn't seem like he had left, only that there was an awkward silence between us. *Maybe God doesn't have good answers for these questions.*

14

ODDS AGAINST ME

Wednesday

Hotel Montana, Port-au-Prince

As long as my mind stayed busy, I didn't think about the hunger. But when my thoughts weren't focused, I could feel the gnawing ache in my stomach. Tension and discomfort joined forces and tied a knot in my gut. How much of it was from missing food, and how much of it was from missing my family? Alone in my dark elevator cave, I wasn't sure I could separate the feelings.

The last time I'd eaten was yesterday at the church. I wished I'd eaten more. Thinking of the church reminded me of the people I'd met. In my mind's eye, I saw the joy on the faces of the moms as they sang worship songs. The rhythms of the songs and the cadence of their foreign words had been mesmerizing. I thought about the boy who slobbered on his mother's shoulder because his candy was too big for his mouth, the girls' beaded hair tinkling as they turned their heads, and the babies who peered out from behind their mothers' skirts. *How many of those moms and babies were still alive?* I pictured the women we filmed and remembered their answers as they described their hopes for their children. I feared that for some of those women, it might be the last image, and perhaps the only image, of them to exist on earth.

Lord, I can't imagine how hard this earthquake has been on Haiti.

Please protect the people of Haiti, especially the poor and the children. Provide for their physical needs, and draw them to you for comfort and grace. Please provide comfort and protection to other survivors who are trapped like we are.

As I prayed, I thought of Missoul and her family. How had the quake impacted them? Were she and her three daughters in the house when the quake hit? I remembered her youngest daughter shaking the Coke can with the rocks in it. Was she playing with that toy when the walls around her started shaking? Had the concrete walls collapsed on them? Or did they get out in time? To get to her house, we had driven nearly thirty miles outside of Port-au-Prince. Were they far enough away to be OK, or were they even closer to the epicenter?

I thought about all the houses on that hillside and on many hillsides in Port-au-Prince. If one house fell, all the rest would come tumbling down. With the force of the quake, it was unlikely any of the houses could have withstood the shaking. Where would families go to get out of the way of the debris landslide? Where would they go if they were hurt? What would they eat? Where would they sleep? The questions haunted me as I pictured the fate of Missoul's once-happy family and then multiplied it times the hundreds of thousands of families just like them in Port-au-Prince. I thought about all of the Haitian men and women who likely spent the night outside, lying in the grass if they were lucky. Lying in the street, if they weren't. I couldn't imagine how many people would be affected. This was the kind of disaster that would impact all sectors of society, but the poor, and especially children, always suffered the most in any disaster.

The sad reality was that for years, the poor in Haiti had been experiencing an ongoing disaster of tragic proportions — rampant poverty, broken infrastructure, corruption, and failed leadership — and then this terrible earthquake struck. Compassion and other organizations had taken care of the poorest of the poor here for years, but an earthquake of this magnitude would exponentially increase the number of people who needed their help.

I thought of the Compassion offices I'd visited on Monday, and the local Compassion staff members I had met there. One of the things that impressed me most was the amount of record keeping these local leaders did. They had a progress record for every child and every mother who'd ever been a part of Compassion's programs. The files were kept in filing cabinets in each church office.

While I was at the church, they opened Missoul's file and had a copy of her baby's footprints and birth certificate. For older children, they had records of spiritual and educational milestones and pictures they'd drawn, and for sponsored children, photocopies of letters between the child and his or her sponsor. Vaccination records, medical records, and church attendance were also included in these files. The Haitian government didn't have records this extensive. In fact, nobody had more information about these poverty-stricken children than Compassion.

If the earthquake separated families or left children without parents, I knew Compassion and their church partners would play a large role in helping to identify and take care of those children. I knew that Compassion employees would take care of their own families first, as they should. But I also knew that after looking after their own families, many of these employees would be back at work within hours, assessing the crisis and going from neighborhood to neighborhood with lists of our children, making sure that every one of them was OK.

I wondered if those children and their families would find some hope in knowing that their names were on a list, a list held by people who cared for them and who would do anything possible to help them through this crisis. The kids enrolled in Compassion's programs would be so much better off than other poor children in Haiti. It made me wish we had enough sponsors for every child living in poverty in this country.

———

Softly at first, then louder as they got closer, I could hear the thawp, thawp, thawp of rotor blades moving across the sky.

"Did you hear that?" I asked Lukeson.

"Hellee-cop-ters!"

Throughout the night, over the past five or six hours, I'd heard only one helicopter fly over. Hearing several at a time gave me hope that we'd made it through the night and that the sun was now up.

"Dan, do you hear the helicopters? Sounds like a couple of them!" yelled Jim.

Were they Haitian or were they from the Dominican Republic? Or maybe they were from the States! It didn't really matter; they were the first solid signs of activity outside of the hotel.

"Are you and your Haitian friend still doing OK?" Jim had been mostly quiet through the night, but this morning I'd overheard him talking with the others and giving Sarla instructions on how to move around the obstacles she'd encountered.

"Yes, we're doing fine. What's going on over there?"

"Sarla sees some light, but she can't get to it yet. We're trying to figure out how she can get there safely."

Initially, I was encouraged by his news, and I relayed the information to Lukeson. But I wondered how much this crack of light really affected our chances of rescue.

The hotel was located at the top of a hill overlooking the city. No one would be near here unless they had to be. We were far from the population center of the city, which was the most natural place for rescuers to start looking for trapped people. But on the positive side, we were at the Hotel Montana. There were visitors from the United States and other countries staying here. Right or wrong, that fact would focus an inordinate amount of attention on this location once rescue operations got under way.

But how would rescuers even get here?

The road up the steep hill to the hotel is a couple of miles long — narrow and winding miles. Each time we'd driven up, I thought we'd never make it, fearing that our SUV might tip over or a wheel would slip off the road and cause us to career down the hill. There was even an incline directly in front of the hotel. Rescuers would need a crane to lift pieces of rubble off the pile, and bulldozers to remove the tons of debris. How would you even get such big pieces of equipment up the hill? And if you could get them up the hill, where would you put a crane so it wouldn't tip on the incline? I thought about other tools they would need — concrete saws and jackhammers. *What if the vibrations from a jackhammer caused already-shaky walls to completely collapse and survival pockets to close?*

While I was encouraged by the sound of the helicopters, I wasn't going to get my hopes up too much. I listened as they flew over us, heading toward the center of the city. The logistics of doing a rescue here were mind-boggling. Though I wasn't an engineer, it didn't look good.

I wasn't ethnocentric enough to think I deserved any special treatment because I was a white American. In fact, I thought quite the opposite. The Haitians would already have so much on their hands that they should pay attention to their own people first. I was a guest in their country, staying where few Haitians could afford to stay. If I was going to be rescued, it was more likely that Americans would rescue me.

I'd heard stories about the Army Corps of Engineers and how good they were at dealing with collapsed buildings and other engineering challenges. I thought about the resources and tools they likely had at their disposal, as well as the talent and experience of their personnel. I wasn't usually a "bring the Americans" type of guy, but that was all I could think of now. *Bring the Americans!* They were physically the closest, the best resourced, and the most experienced. My best hope of being rescued was by Americans. But I wasn't going to lie around and wait. I didn't want to die in the elevator without at least trying to get out.

I had put the journal back in my pants pocket. If I died, it would be found on my body, but I still didn't want my body to be found curled up in a ball at the bottom of an elevator without having done anything to get myself out.

Father, I don't want to die here in the elevator without trying to escape. So I'm thinking of climbing this elevator shaft. Please give me ideas and wisdom. Help me to know when to make the attempt — or not.

Using the handrail, I once again pulled myself up. I took my camera and hopped on my right leg to the elevator opening. Just as I'd done when I first arrived in the elevator, I pointed the light of the camera up into the shaft above me. Because the elevator had shifted away from the walls of the shaft during the quake, there was a small gap between the shaft and the outside wall of the elevator car. It looked as though I could squeeze up into the gap. I couldn't see how far up the shaft went. *It would be a crazy, radical, and wonderful thing if the shaft had stayed intact.* I could just climb to the top and come out above the rubble pile, then just walk down off the pile. *But that could be dangerous if the pile was shifting. Maybe I'd just sit on top of the rubble, waving to people who went by and saying, "Hey rescuers, I'm up here!"*

If I couldn't find my way out of the shaft, at least I would see if I could get a signal on my phone. At some point, the cell towers would be restored. But even if they were up and functioning, it wasn't very likely I would get a signal from where I was now, underneath so much concrete debris. However, if I was in the shaft, and especially if there was a hole somewhere in the shaft, then I could call Christy and Compassion and tell them where I was.

But how would I climb it?

My left leg was broken and had a big gash, but other than that, I was in OK shape. But I wasn't currently all that athletic, and I knew I wasn't strong enough to pull myself up by my arms alone. *What if I used a combination of legs and arms?* If I could push up with my right leg — and I'd probably have to risk using my left leg some — I could use my arms to pull myself up the rest of the way. If I could get on top of the elevator car, it would just be a matter of climbing as high as I could until I got a cell phone signal or found a way to get out.

I shut off the camera and groped my way back to my spot in the elevator. In the dark, I thought through my plan. Could I really do it? Is there any chance it would work? Before I did anything, I needed to think through all of the details.

If they found my body in Haiti, I wanted Christy to know that I did everything I could to get out alive.

I wished I could share the plan with her. I was sure she could improve it or tell me how to fix it. I often brought my ideas and plans home from work to get her creative input or critique. I teased her, calling her my "personal focus group." Her intuitive instincts were usually just what I needed to take my ideas to the next level, or to realize that I should go back to the drawing board. *I wonder what she'd tell me now.*

"It's too risky, Dan," I could almost hear her voice warning me. "Just hang on until rescuers come, Love." I pictured her face, with the depth of empathy and love that her eyes would express in a moment like this. I longed for her touch and cried, thinking we'd probably never comfort each other again.

15

A SAVIOR

From what I could comprehend, Sarla was forcing herself to crawl in total darkness over piles of rubble, groping her way along as she inched around on her hands and knees exploring various openings.

"How's Sarla doing?" I asked Jim.

"She's trying to work her way to the outside of the building," Jim said, "but she keeps getting turned around and then gets confused about where she is."

Listening to her conversation with Jim, I could tell that she was an intelligent, well-educated woman. I guessed middle-aged. She seemed to be slightly claustrophobic, and I was concerned that she seemed tentative about exploring new openings. Not that I blamed her; she was crawling around in the pitch-black.

"Can she get close to you?" I asked Jim.

"Yes, she can see our cell phones' lights through the cracks in the walls."

"Is there any chance you could pass her one of your cell phones?"

"We already tried that. She couldn't reach them."

Jim addressed Sarla again. "See if you can climb through that hole you went through a while ago. Maybe you can see some daylight now."

I listened as she responded to Jim. "I see a little bit of light off in the distance."

"Can you get to it?" Jim asked.

"I don't know. I don't think so."

"Well, do you think you could try? I don't want you to do anything that puts you in danger, so be really careful, but do you think you could try?"

"I'll try."

I crossed my fingers and whispered a prayer. Jim and the others were trapped next to the registration desk and had no access to the outside world. Lukeson was sealed in his elevator car. I had access to a bit of the lobby in front of the elevator, but the area was completely enclosed, and there was no way to get out of the confined space. Unless our cell phones suddenly started working, Sarla was our only possible connection to the outside world.

Her voice sounded anxious, pinched. "I can't. There's a big ledge in my way."

I could hear Jim gently coaxing her. "Can you pull yourself up onto it?"

"I don't know. I'm afraid I might fall."

"I don't want you to get hurt. Just pull up on it with a little bit of weight and see if it holds." The conversation continued between Jim and Sarla until she was convinced that the ledge would hold her weight. She pulled herself up onto it and then worked her way down the other side.

Even though I had become familiar with my surroundings, I found the darkness scary. I couldn't imagine what it felt like to be moving through unknown places, getting turned around and fearing you might never make it back. I pictured her on top of a ledge and wondered what it would feel like not to know what was on the other side and whether she could slide to the floor, jump down, or possibly even fall to her death.

"I'm in a new spot, but I see at least one more area I have to cross before I can reach the light."

"Can you keep going?" Jim asked.

"Yes, I'm trying." Hearing the emotion in her voice, I again prayed for her safety.

As Jim and the others encouraged Sarla's journey toward the

light, I thought it was a perfect time to continue my conversation with Lukeson. We'd talked a bit, but he had been quiet during the night. And, of course, I'd been lost in my own thoughts while writing notes in my journal. However, since we heard the helicopters overhead, Lukeson had been more active, and I was relieved to hear him moving around in his elevator.

"Lukeson, one of Jim's friends sees light. She can move around, and she's trying to get to it to see if she can attract some attention."

"Dat's very good, Dan-yell."

"But even though Sarla can move around, she can't rescue us. We need someone from the outside to come and get us out."

"Dat's very true, Dan-yell."

"I thought about climbing up the elevator shaft to see if I could get a signal."

"A signal?"

"On my cell phone."

"Oh."

"Even if I got a signal and contacted someone, I still couldn't save us by myself. We need someone from the outside to come and save us." Some of our conversation was made difficult by the language barrier, but I continued to try. "We can't get out of this building by our own efforts. With all of the concrete floors above us, the only way we'll be rescued is if rescuers reach down from above the debris and pull us out. I could take off my shoe and bang it against the wall and hope I would eventually force my way out, but the walls are too thick. It's beyond my ability to pound my way out. We need a rescuer. We need a savior."

"Yes, dat's true."

"That's what Jesus has done for us. He is our Savior, our rescuer. By ourselves we can't overcome our sins or be good enough to get to heaven. It's like me climbing a little way up the shaft, but not the whole way."

"A little way does no good."

"That's right! We need Jesus to come and save us. If Jesus hadn't come as a rescuer from above, we would have no hope of getting right with God and reaching heaven."

"And last night he saved *me*, Dan-yell."

"Yes, Lukeson. Yes he did." He had understood.

Throughout my conversation with Lukeson, I could hear Jim and the others talking excitedly. At a break in our conversation, I asked if Sarla had made any more progress. "Hey, Jim, what's going on?"

"Sarla sees the light source. It's a hole in one of the walls. She thinks she can get closer to it."

"Is it big enough for her to crawl through?"

"No, I don't think so."

"Keep me posted."

"Will do."

I turned my attention back to Lukeson and talked with him about ways he could grow in his newfound faith. I explained that the Bible contains God's words for us and that it reveals the story of God's rescue plan through Jesus. I suggested that he start reading the gospel of John because for many people that was an easy place to start. I explained how accepting Jesus meant he was giving up his right to control his life; instead, he was choosing to live his life according to what the Bible says is right and wrong.

We discussed how prayer was like a conversation with God and how through prayer he could ask what God wanted him to do and who God wanted him to be.

"If we get out of here, Lukeson, try to find a Christian church and introduce yourself to someone in that church. Tell them what you did."

"That I accepted Jee-sus?"

"Yes."

"I will, Dan-yell."

If we made it out alive, I wondered what Lukeson would be returning to. Would he still have a home? Would his fiancée and his mother still be alive? I was hopeful he would be able to connect with a church and the people in it. Through a combination of Jesus and a church body in his life — a community of believers — the difference would be significant, regardless of what he found when he got out of this rubble pile. I wondered what an impact he could make in his home and his community as a new follower of Jesus.

I thought I heard a muted voice in the distance. I stopped talking long enough to listen. It was Sarla timidly yelling. *What was she doing?*

Throughout the night, I had heard Jim and the others trying to draw attention to our situation by coordinating their banging. Someone, usually Jim, would count "One, two, three!" Then they would all begin banging on the walls and yelling "Help!" as loudly as they could. Once I figured out what they were doing, I joined in, pounding on the elevator shaft and yelling as loudly as I could. Lukeson also added his voice.

I listened to Sarla desperately trying to make her voice heard, and I wondered if we all needed to help her.

"What's going on with Sarla?" I asked Jim.

"She can hear voices. She's trying to get their attention."

She needs to yell louder than that. I knew I shouldn't be critical. Sarla, like the rest of us, was doing the best she could. "Can she reach through the crack?"

"I don't know. I'll check."

I could hear Jim communicating with her, but I couldn't hear her response. "Yes, she can get her hand out, but that's all."

"Ask her if she can bang on something or throw rocks to get their attention." I tried to think of what else I could suggest that might help her get noticed. "Can she wave something? Maybe a piece of her clothing?"

"Wait, she's made contact with someone."

She made contact with someone? I could hear Jim and Sarla talking back and forth. I tried not to get excited, but I could feel my pulse racing. When there was a pause in their conversation, Jim confirmed that Sarla had made contact with an outside person.

"She just told him there are six Americans who are trapped and need help."

Six? She must be thinking of herself and the four trapped with Jim.

111

I heard Sarla's voice timidly yelling in the distance. I could make out a bit of her side of the conversation, but I couldn't hear if anyone replied.

"Did he say anything?"

There was further exchange between Jim and Sarla, of which I could only hear Jim's half. I was vicariously living an adventure that was completely out of my control.

"He responded in Creole," Jim said, "but Sarla didn't understand what he said. Ann and I repeated the message in French, and the man said, 'OK' — and then we heard his footsteps leaving. Sounds good, Dan. Sounds like he's going for help!"

I smiled in the dark. I had talked myself into believing it would take days to be found by a rescuer, *if* we were ever discovered. But now, in just hours, through Sarla, we've made contact with the outside world! There was still a lot that needed to happen before we were actually free, but my spirits lifted, because this was the first real sign of progress. Had I been sitting up, I would have done a fist pump. I was absolutely elated.

I shared the good news with Lukeson. "Looks like someone is going to try and rescue us." I rubbed my neck, I hadn't realized until now how much I'd been affected by the weight of all that I'd been carrying — physically and mentally.

"That's great, Dan-yell. That's great."

"Is Sarla going to wait for him to return?" I asked Jim.

"Yes, she's been working all night. Now she's going to sit by the hole and rest while she waits for him to come back."

"Please tell her thank you for me. She is a very brave woman!"

I heard Jim relay my message. Despite the pain that his friends were in, I could hear happy talk from several of the voices on Jim's side of the lobby.

Hope was a beautiful thing to see. Even in the darkness.

DanWoolley.net (all photos)

BEAUTY AND POVERTY IN HAITI—IN LIVING COLOR

During my first day in Port-au-Prince, I sensed that the Haitian people were defying the weight of oppressive poverty with color, vitality, and passion for life. Flamboyant tap-taps (above)—cars, trucks, and buses converted into overcrowded taxis—showcased some of Haiti's festive artwork.

I took this picture of hillside slums from my room at the Hotel Montana on Tuesday morning, January 12. Even before the earthquake, I was struck by how fragile these buildings looked, stacked on top of one another like a giant game of Jenga.

RESCUING MOMS AND BABIES

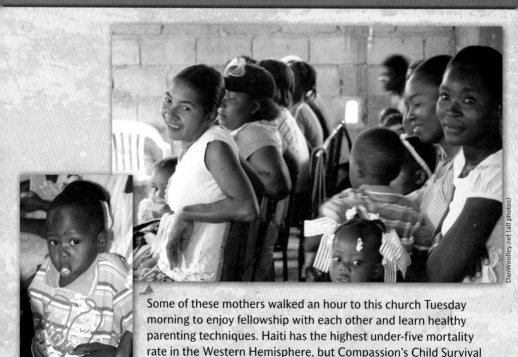

DanWoolley.net (all photos)

Some of these mothers walked an hour to this church Tuesday morning to enjoy fellowship with each other and learn healthy parenting techniques. Haiti has the highest under-five mortality rate in the Western Hemisphere, but Compassion's Child Survival Program will ensure that these vulnerable children will survive and have opportunities to break the cycle of poverty.

Defend the cause of the weak and fatherless; maintain the rights of the poor and oppressed. Rescue the weak and needy.

Psalm 82:3–4a

I was so glad to be living out my faith in this way!

We spent Tuesday afternoon at the house of Missoul, one of the moms in Compassion's Child Survival Program. Her two older daughters had mental disabilities caused by malnutrition while she was pregnant, but her youngest was healthy because of Compassion's intervention. It was great to see the love she showed to her daughters; here Micheleine is playing with an improvised Coke can rattle (right).

DanWoolley.net (all photos)

FROM EXTREME POVERTY

THE HOTEL MONTANA BEFORE...

Hôtel Montana Haïti

After another hotel lost my reservation, I was booked at the Hotel Montana, a beautiful respite with stunning views of Port-au-Prince (top). This view of the front of the hotel (middle) shows the full six-story height above the lobby.

AND AFTER

▲ The 7.0 earthquake struck at 4:53 p.m. on Tuesday, January 12. Though the quake reportedly lasted 35 seconds, it took just 3 seconds for the Montana to collapse completely.

I took these pictures a few minutes after the earthquake while I tried to make sense of my surroundings and seek safety in the darkness. The joint where the partially fallen ceiling met the lobby wall (below) looked very unstable, so I debated whether to risk crawling to the open elevator (left).

DanWoolley.net (top and right)

UNDER THE MONTANA

Lukeson's elevator was also miraculously on the lobby floor, but with its door stuck closed. The concrete slab to the right is part of the ceiling that missed me by inches.

Sam Gray / Virginia Task Force One

The view from my elevator (when I flashed the camera). In the first minutes after the quake, I was crouched down with my foot pinned by debris on the other side of the fallen white support beam. I left a trail of blood as I crawled twenty feet to the open elevator car. Seconds after I reached it, a 6.0 aftershock struck, and I heard another wall fall where I was originally pinned.

Sam Gray / Virginia Task Force One

65 HOURS IN A BROKEN ELEVATOR

This was how my elevator ► looked after my 65-hour ordeal (I didn't leave it better than I found it – sorry, Mom). The wall is stained from my efforts to stop the bleeding of my head wound with my sock. This elevator became my sanctuary, and I felt that God was with me in the darkness.

Where can I go from your Spirit, O Lord. Where can I flee from your presence... If I make my bed in the depths, you are there.
Psalm 139:7, 8

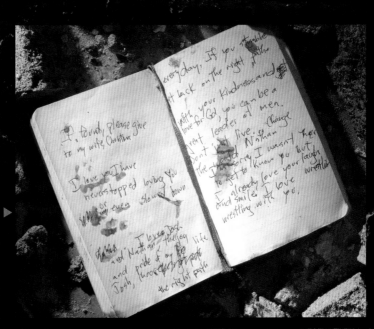

Not sure whether I would survive and be rescued, I thought a lot about my wife and kids. I wrote notes to them in a journal in the dark, hoping my scribbles would be legible despite smudges of blood and tears. ▶

DanWoolley.net

DESTRUCTION IN HAITI

While I was fighting to survive, the city of Port-au-Prince was reeling from one of the most destructive natural disasters in history. I took this picture (left) on Monday. I never could have imagined that the Presidential Palace would be destroyed the next day, along with an estimated 70 percent of the city's buildings.

▼

DanWoolley.net

Tim Glenn / Compassion International – Compassion.com / unshaken (left and above)

▲

Poorly crafted and enforced construction codes caused failures of buildings across economic lines, turning a frightening natural disaster into an inconceivable human tragedy. Add a lack of access to emergency and medical services after the quake, and it is clear that poverty is the primary reason the death toll in Haiti rose to an estimated 230,000.

In the first days after the quake, Haitians worked heroically to rescue survivors with few tools.

With so many homes destroyed and aftershocks terrorizing survivors, millions spent the first weeks in tent cities, unable or afraid to return to their homes. Children and the poor always suffer the most when disasters strike.

RESCUE EFFORTS AT THE HOTEL MONTANA

▲ The roof of the Montana collapsed to within inches of the ground in the roundabout in front of the lobby. The bent elevator shaft is to the far left (see photo on the next page).

▲ Members of the search and rescue team from Fairfax, VA, digging under the Montana

In some places, the "pancaked" floors of the Montana were separated by mere inches. ▶

Sarla Chand (left), Jim Gulley (below), and two of their colleagues were rescued late Thursday night by a French rescue team. When sounds of rescue diminished after they were removed, I wondered if I had been forgotten.

U.S. Navy Photo by Mass Communication Specialist First Class Joshua Lee Kelsey

AFP / Getty Images

Sam Gray, part of a search and rescue team from Fairfax, VA, saw the elevator shaft that bent perpendicular two stories up from the lobby (above) and wondered if he could find survivors in the elevators. Their team cut this hole (right) in a maintenance panel to facilitate my rescue.

Mark Plunkett / Virginia Task Force One

Brian Gillingham / Virginia Task Force One

MY RESCUE

Though I didn't take this picture (top), this is how I remember seeing Sam when he came down the elevator shaft to rescue me. An hour or so later, strapped into an orange stretcher (right), I passed through this Hall of Heroes (below) as they pulled me through the debris-filled elevator shaft to safety.

Mark Plunkett / Virginia Task Force One (left and above)

Find rest, O my soul, in God alone; my hope comes from him. He alone is my rock and my salvation; he is my fortress, I will not be shaken.

Psalm 62:5-6

I'll never forget the first moment I felt the sun on my face — I was going home! Lukeson, with a rescuer (right), was clearly in better shape than I was after getting some food and water.

Front cover photo: Lukeson placing his hand on my face the moment we saw each other for the first time.

My rescuers from Fairfax, VA. Back row, left to right: William Moreland, Mike Davis, Carlos Carrillo, George Hahn, Sam Gray, Evan Lewis, Brian Gillingham, Buck Best. Front row, left to right: Eddie Thurston, Daryl Casey, Doc MacIntyre, Teresa MacPherson, and Banks the rescue dog.

Two beautiful mornings in my life—reunited with Christy as I recovered in a Miami hospital (above), and my first morning at home in Colorado with Nathan and Josh, one week after the quake

GOING HOME

The Woolley family, September 2010: May you experience God's presence and grace as you face earthquakes big and small in your life. Please continue to pray for the people of Haiti.

16

DOUBTS

1997

Monrovia, California

Four years into our marriage, the depression was still with us. We had just finished a quiet dinner and were standing together at the sink drying dishes. Christy hadn't said much during the meal. I watched as she slowly wiped the rim of a glass. Though she wasn't crying, I could see the sadness in her eyes — a mixture of pain and hopelessness. Her eyes were those of someone mourning a profound loss.

She looked up and saw me staring. "How long will this sadness last?"

"What?"

"Another year? Two years? How long will we have to live like this?" She placed the glass in the cupboard and picked up another one.

"I don't know, Christy, but we *will* get past this."

"I can't see it. I can't see our future. There's no hope anything will ever get better."

I took the glass from her cold hands and set it on the table. "Come here," I said pulling her close to me. I tightened my arms around her. "We're making a lot of progress in counseling. I'm looking forward to our future, when we've moved beyond this to another stage of our

113

lives." I rested my chin on top of her head. "Can I share something I was reading this morning?"

I walked to the sofa and sat down, and she sat down next to me. My Bible was on the table, and I flipped to Jeremiah 29:11 and read aloud a verse we were both familiar with. " 'For I know the plans I have for you,' declares the LORD, 'plans to prosper you and not to harm you, plans to give you hope and a future.' "

After several long minutes she quietly spoke up. "I don't believe that anymore."

I stared at her, unsure of what to say.

"How *can* I believe it?" She turned to look at me. "These promises seem like hollow, empty words. I *feel* harmed." She stood up and walked to the window. "I don't feel any *hope*, and I can't see a *future* — at least not a future I can live through."

"God is going to come through for us, Christy. We both know there are so many promises in the Bible that tell us how God cares for his children. We need to have faith in those promises," I said in as gentle a tone as I could muster.

"I don't think he's going to make things better. Just look at our lives, Dan."

"Can we pray together? Can we talk with God about how you're feeling?" I expected her to walk back to the sofa. Instead, she didn't move.

"I can't pray."

"OK, I'll just pray for us."

"Fine. Do whatever you want." I looked up to see her turn from the window and walk to the bedroom.

I sat there, the Bible open in my lap, wondering what to do next.

———

Over the next few months, Christy's melancholy seemed even deeper. She was sad and frustrated with the apparent lack of progress. I knew there were times she wanted to give up on life, on me, and on our marriage.

"You should divorce me. I've changed so much — I'm not the person you married. You deserve better, and I'm just holding you back."

When she said the *D* word, I yelled at her. "We are not going to give up on our marriage!" I calmed myself down and changed my tone. "I'm sorry. I'm really sorry I yelled at you." I moved in front of her so I could look in her eyes, but she looked away.

Divorce had come up before, and I almost always yelled at her when it did, though I knew how unhelpful and even ironic that response was. We were trying so hard to get through the depression that the thought of giving up the battle or giving up on our marriage angered me. Whenever she suggested divorce as a solution, I felt like *I* had failed.

Christy couldn't understand why I wanted to stay married to her, and she thought it would be better for me if I let her go. In her mind, she thought I could find happiness with someone else — and that way, at least *one* of us would be happy. But divorce wasn't an acceptable solution for me. Christy was the love of my life.

"I'm not ready to give up on us, Christy, and it makes me mad to even think about it. Will you please forgive me for yelling?" Whether she really forgave me or just didn't have the stomach for a fight, she seemed ready to move on. I touched her gently on the cheek, and she looked up at me.

"Christy, I didn't marry and fall in love with an abstract idea of you. I love *you*." I put my finger on her heart. "The you deep inside who is suffering right now. The you who is sad because you don't feel like yourself. I didn't choose to live my life with a mannequin or robot who will always look and act exactly the same as the day we fell in love. I chose to give my love to a living, breathing, changing, growing, declining, advancing, flawed-yet-wonderful woman whom I will love through all the stages of our lives. For better or for worse, in sickness and in health, till death do us part. I am with you, forever and always, Christy."

She looked into my eyes with that deep searching look that seemed like she wanted to read my heart. The tension in her face softened, and her tears started flowing. Her crying turned to sobbing.

I embraced her, glad to see her open her heart a little to accept my love, even if opening her heart meant experiencing the sadness more deeply. I wept with her, and my heart broke as I thought of the depth of her suffering.

———

Christy and I were growing more isolated. We knew we needed the support of friends and family in our lives, but we found it hard to be open with others about what we were going through.

I believed people around us genuinely cared, but when they asked how we were doing and we answered honestly, they often didn't know how to respond. Many offered instant solutions like, "You just need to find a hobby"; shared platitudes like, "God won't give you more than you can handle"; and familiar Bible verses that weren't always helpful in the drive-by way they were tossed to us.

I'm sure these friends and acquaintances hoped their quick statements of encouragement would help in some way, but at times I felt these efforts were more about fending off the awkwardness of talking about suffering. No one likes to talk about pain.

We were so grateful for the rare times when a friend or church acquaintance would hear about the trial we were living through and respond with genuine sadness and concern. These empathetic people would say something like, "Oh, I am so very sorry for what you are dealing with," and then open the door to further conversation or offer to help in any way they could. Without trying to solve it, they entered into our pain, ready to suffer with us. But these people were rare, and this response was the exception, so we mostly found ourselves isolated from those around us.

Earlier in our marriage, Christy and I both saw church as a core part of our spiritual lives, as an important opportunity for encouragement and fellowship with other followers of Christ. We had looked forward to hearing teaching from Scripture, worshiping God together, and learning from others about their journeys of faith.

But as we got deeper into the depression hole, church became more difficult for us. Sometimes it was the worship time that was difficult. It was hard to sing "This is the day that the Lord has made; we will rejoice and be glad in it" — a song we had liked at other times in our lives — when we felt light-years away from that sentiment. *Where were the songs that aligned with our suffering and helped us cry out to God in our pain?*

We started exploring other Christian churches to see if we could find one that ministered more to our situation. Ironically, the upbeat atmosphere at most churches was challenging for us. We tried to be authentic and open, but we didn't find a natural outlet to share our pain. When we did share with others, we were often faced with the standard quick-fix answers. We felt like we had to make a choice: be true to our hurting selves and stand out, or put on our happy, "normal" faces and pass through with less attention. Christy found that faking a public persona took energy she didn't have. To appear "normal" on Sunday, she had to borrow energy from the days ahead, and then she'd spend the rest of the week repaying it.

One church we visited had a pastor who was sadly misguided. During his sermon he said, "If you find yourself depressed, don't waste time with medication or a counselor. The problem is sin in your life and your lack of true faith in God." His words were incredibly painful to Christy. Plus, he was wrong. Yes, sin can contribute to depression, and both of us are quick to admit that we are sinners. But there are so many factors that contribute to depression, and there is not one simplistic solution. Telling Christy to give up her counseling and medication didn't make sense. *Would this pastor tell a diabetic to give up insulin and doctor visits?*

We knew that church was an important part of a growing and sustaining faith, but we reached a point where we gave up on church. As time went on, reading Scripture or devotional books and praying together became difficult, so I continued on my own. Though Christy had posted Bible verses around the house for encouragement, by this time she had stopped any regular Bible reading or devotional time.

I began to see declines in my own devotional life as well. In the early days of our marriage, I found encouragement from God almost every day: in Scripture, during prayer times, or through conversations with Christy or friends. But as the years passed, some months felt completely devoid of God's presence.

I began to get impatient with God.

Why are you letting this happen? Why are we going through all of this?

I was trying to hold on to faith for both of us, but I was growing increasingly frustrated with God and turning to him less. We weren't going to church. We weren't reading the Bible together. We found it hard to trust God's promises. What if we reached a point where the depression dragged us away from our core beliefs? Where would we be then?

Things were bad now, but they could still get much worse.

I trembled at the thought.

17

GET HELP

Wednesday

Hotel Montana, Port-au-Prince

Several hours had passed since Sarla had made contact with the outsider, and there had been no further activity. Worry started pushing back the hope I had felt. "Has Sarla heard anything yet?" I asked for the umpteenth time. I felt like a kid on a road trip who kept asking his parents, "Are we there yet?"

Like that kid, I knew the answer even before Jim replied. "Not yet."

"Maybe they can't find her location? Perhaps we should start banging again?"

A couple of times on Tuesday night through Wednesday morning, we'd all simultaneously yelled and banged on the walls, hoping to attract attention. But since Sarla's brief connection with the outside world, we hadn't done it again. Now that it was daylight, it seemed we had a better chance of someone hearing us.

Jim agreed.

I grabbed a piece of concrete that was small enough to fit in my hand but big enough to whack the elevator wall and make a noise

Jim counted us off. "Here we go! One, two, three. Helllp!"

We all joined in the racket. We banged and yelled for thirty to forty-five seconds, then paused to catch our breath before repeating.

119

We knew we were under a lot of concrete and other debris, but we wanted to do whatever we could to let people know we were there. It didn't seem like it should take as much effort as it did, but each time we finished I was panting as if I had just run a grueling mile.

From that point on, we banged and yelled at least once every hour. Sometimes we would say different things: "We're here!" Or, "We have injuries!" A couple of times I heard one of the men trapped with Jim yell, "We're Americans." Or, "We have money!"

I thought that was interesting. I never yelled that one, but I understood his point. If we could attract the attention of a Haitian who needed money and was willing to dig us out with his bare hands, well then, so be it. I'd gladly pay him everything I had with me. More if he wanted it. But I also wondered if shouting "We're Americans" could backfire on us. Not everyone thinks as highly of our country as we do.

As the afternoon passed, we banged four or five more times with no results. By then, it had been at least eight hours since Sarla had contacted the outsider, which meant it had to be late afternoon or early evening. It seemed clear he wasn't coming back.

I was finding it hard to sit or lie in one place for longer than ten minutes at a time. Cramped airline seats were uncomfortable, but not being able to stretch out in the elevator for so many hours was excruciating. The pieces of debris pressing against my flesh and especially against my bones sent sharp pains through my back and hips until I moved them to another uncomfortable position. I had to shift often, and, of course, that meant that each time I moved, I had to brush away bits of debris to clear a spot for me to rest. While wiping some of the smaller rocks out of the elevator, I felt something unusual. It was a thin cylinder. Too round to be debris, it had to be man-made.

My pen!

It was the original pen I'd lost the night before. *Thank you, God!* I knew many of the notes I'd written with my Sharpie must be illegible, and I welcomed a chance to make them more readable. Since I had less than one bar left on the battery in my camera, I used the light from my phone to help me go back through the pages of my journal. As much as possible I tried to clean up my notes to make sure they were legible. I also thought of a few more practical things I wanted to tell Christy, and I added them to the book.

When I finished, I tucked my pen safely in my pants pocket. I didn't want to take a chance of losing it again. But as I slid it in, it snagged on something. I reached in and pulled out a package of gum. *How had I missed this?* There were two pieces left.

I sniffed the mint gum and licked my lips in anticipation. I recalled how cool the taste of a fresh piece of gum felt. As a child, I'd been told not to swallow gum, but like all kids, I'd done it more than once. I remembered the feeling that chewed gum made in my stomach. It was like a lump. While I knew the gum had no nutritional value, I welcomed the opportunity to chew it and remove some of the concrete paste and nasty taste from my mouth. I even welcomed the lump of gum in my empty stomach.

As I popped the Chiclets-style gum out of its wrapper, the minty smell was a breath of freshness. I put the gum in my mouth and allowed the flavor to spread. I slowly started to chew.

Even before I could get the gum softened, I realized I'd made a mistake. The gum whisked all of the moisture out of my mouth. I snatched it from my mouth and wanted to fling it out of the elevator, but I knew that was stupid. *I need to save it — it might come in handy.* I had started a small stash of resources in one corner of the elevator, though I didn't know how or when I might use them. I added the rectangular, cardboard gum container to my stash and stuck the chewed piece of gum on the wall above my head so I could find it if I needed it.

I stopped moving when I heard Jim's voice. "Maybe they aren't able to rescue us." He was talking to the others who were trapped with him.

"What if they had no intention of helping us?"

"Maybe they were just here to see what was left of the hotel."

"They didn't seem like rescuers."

"Jim?" I wanted him to know I could hear his conversation.

"It doesn't look good, Dan."

121

I paused. Now that Jim said out loud what I'd been thinking, my hope was sucked away. There had to be something I could do.

When I had mentioned my idea of climbing out the elevator shaft to Jim earlier, he pointed out that my leg would be a problem. But I had been thinking about it more since then, and I was trying to develop a plan where I wouldn't need to use my injured leg so much. But it had also occurred to me that it would be dark when I climbed into the shaft. I'd have to find a way to affix my iPhone to my head like a miner's lamp so my hands would be free to climb.

It was risky. I could fall, or something could fall on me. But it looked as if it might be my only choice — our only choice — to be found and rescued. I didn't say anything else to Jim about my dangerous plan, but now I had a name for it. It was my "endgame plan." I would do it when there was no hope of being rescued but before I got too weak to execute it. It would be my last effort. I only hoped that I would live through it and not die trying.

I thought about the outsider that Sarla had made contact with; he obviously wasn't coming back. I didn't know who he was or what his story was, but I just wished that rather than disappearing, he would have told someone, anyone, who could have helped us.

Or, maybe he did tell someone.

What if he told someone, and they wouldn't — or couldn't — come?

Maybe when Sarla told them there were six, that wasn't enough. If she had included Lukeson and me in the total, would that have made a difference? Or perhaps it was just too hard to get the rescue equipment up to the hotel.

The continuous banging had worn me out and stirred up more concrete powder in the elevator. As the dust caked in my mouth, I realized I was becoming dehydrated.

As morning turned into afternoon, I wondered how much longer I could last. I decided to use the remaining battery in the camera to leave final messages for my family. I wrote:

Wednesday.

I think I will likely pass to heaven tonight or tomorrow. The rescuers have not returned — likely too difficult a rescue and too many other, easier needs.

If I die know that I fell asleep without pain.

I wasn't being totally truthful. Of course I was in pain — just not in the agony I thought I should have been in. So it was true that if I died, I didn't die an agonizingly painful death. I knew Christy would imagine my body bloodied, broken, and forgotten. When certain things got into her mind, sometimes it was hard for her to get them out. I didn't want her obsessing over the pain I was in when I died. I didn't want her to have that image or those thoughts.

I ♥ you all.

I thought about David's family learning about his death. He had died instantly and without pain. I hoped it would be comforting in at least a small way. Thoughts of that last moment played in my mind. Me lunging toward the outdoors, David lunging — but the picture changed. As I imagined his final step, I imagined him lunging straight into the arms of Jesus. It was as if Jesus was standing on the threshold of heaven with his arms open wide, just waiting to catch him. The thought brought me a bittersweet joy. Jesus was there for him, and I knew he'd be there to catch me too.

Still, the question of *good* lingered for me. How could any of this be good? How could I long for heaven when I ached to be with my wife and boys?

We had some friends who were particularly sensitive to emotional issues. I wrote a note to Christy asking her to seek their help and encouragement. Then I wrote a note to them that stated:

Watch over her emotional state. Make sure she gets into counseling.

My battery had been blinking for a while, telling me it was past low. Before it went out, the last words I wrote to Christy were:

Don't give up: really work at faith in Christ.
Despite my failings — my issues, not yours —
you, Christy, were loved by a man
who was madly in love with you and only you.
I will always love you.

18

FUTURE FLASHES

The pressure in my bladder had been increasing to the point I could no longer deny it — I had to go again. But I had learned my lesson; this time I wasn't going to use my shirt. I took another inventory of my resources: a journal, a pen, a Sharpie, a passport, a cardboard gum package, an iPhone, and a camera. What could I use to catch the urine?

I considered my camera, but I didn't know if it contained chemicals that could cause me harm if I used it as a cup. I felt a little like MacGyver, but I wished I were fashioning some type of explosive to punch a hole out of here instead of the challenge I was facing.

Of the few resources I had, I realized my journal held the most potential as a cup. I carefully tore a piece of paper from the back. If I could fashion some kind of cone, perhaps I could make it work. But my attempts at elevator origami weren't yielding the results I desired. I found myself wishing I had my backpack. There were two water bottles hanging off the side, and using one of those bottles would make it so much easier.

I chuckled to myself for even thinking such a thing. If I'd had those water bottles, I could drink the water in them and wouldn't need a receptacle for my urine! Still, it would be much easier to urinate in a bottle. As I continued to bend and fold the paper, trying to fashion some type of cup, I realized it would never work. The paper was too flimsy, and once wet, it would immediately disintegrate.

The cardboard pack of gum!

I found the discarded package in the corner of the elevator and peeled off the cardboard sleeve. By ripping the edge and refolding it, I was able to form a cup. I reached above me and felt for the gum I had placed there earlier. I grabbed it and used it to seal the edge. Now I had a cup. MacGyver would be proud.

Using the handrail on the back of the elevator, I hauled myself up so I was standing. Then I gingerly took a couple of steps toward the elevator opening. Once in place, I attempted to fill the cup. Despite the inefficiency of my methods, I caught some urine. I then raised the cup to my lips and drank the warm liquid.

This time, the experience wasn't just unpleasant; it was staggering. I wasn't sure if it was because my urine was more concentrated after not drinking anything for so long or if it was because I didn't filter it through my T-shirt, but the acrid taste caught me off guard. I gagged. Still, I forced myself to choke it down. If this was what it took to stay alive, I didn't care. I'd do whatever I needed to.

When finished, I made my way back to my spot and lay down. I folded the cup and put it back in the corner with my other supplies. If I lasted another day, I could use it again.

———

I wanted to sleep, but I couldn't because my mind was racing. One minute I was holding fast to my faith; the next, my doubts so overwhelmed me that it took all my willpower to continue to believe anything good. I was torn up emotionally by the questions racking my brain.

If I died in Haiti, Christy might kill herself.

It wasn't the only possible outcome, but it was the outcome I feared most. Whether it happened in a week, in a year, or in ten years, I feared that hearing the news of my death might put into motion her descent into depression — only this time, I wouldn't be there to help her out of it.

That was the worst-case scenario, and I found my mind lingering on this possibility.

If that didn't happen, what would her life be like? When she was healthy and when I was there to help, she handled life beautifully. She was a good mother and a creative teacher, and the boys loved being homeschooled. In the evenings and on weekends, I was there to give her a break and help out with chores.

But how would she manage without help?

And without an income?

I knew she'd have to quit homeschooling and get a job. Christy would hate that. As the primary teacher for our boys, she felt she was giving them the best education they could get. Having to give up schooling the boys would gravely disappoint her. In addition, having to work at a job all day and come home to take care of the boys without any help would physically thrash her. She'd be exhausted *every day*. Between her disappointment, exhaustion, sadness, and perhaps anger at my death, she faced potentially insurmountable emotional odds on a daily basis. It was hard to imagine good coming out of that for Christy.

Likewise, if the boys lost me and if Christy had to go back to work, how would that affect them? I wanted to be there to help nurture their character. Would someone step in to help Christy with their character development? Their grandpa would be there as a positive male role model, but would other men step in as well?

My life experience had taught me not to settle. I wanted more than an average life for my boys. I didn't want them paying lukewarm lip service to God and attending church out of habit. I wanted them to live fully — zealous for life and passionate for God. I didn't want them to grow up and just get whatever job they could. I wanted them to find a career they loved and contribute in a way that made a positive impact on the world.

Could God make these things happen without me being a part of their lives? Could God make good come from my death? Intellectually, I would say that he could.

But I still didn't have the faith to believe it.

I had read enough survival stories to know that remaining positive was critical to surviving; but as negative thoughts continued to flood my mind, I realized I was losing hope. Intellectually, I had always understood what Christy went through as she wrestled with despair during her depression, but for the first time I *felt* it.

I tried to recall how Christy had battled her negative thoughts, and I remembered one particular strategy. She took objects — mementos from happier days, pictures and items in which she found beauty — and placed them where she could see them to remind her of God's love for her. Later as a couple, we would place reminders of our blessings and answered prayers in prominent locations as a way to honor God's faithfulness to us.

We continued this practice after we had kids. We chose a basket, and whenever there was an answered prayer we wanted to remember — about health issues, financial needs, or even spiritual milestones — we put a rock in the basket, along with a note that reminded us of what God had done. We called this our Jordan Basket, referring to the Old Testament story about Joshua, who built a memorial along-side the Jordan River.

I decided to do something similar in the elevator. I cleared a small spot along one wall and placed a three-inch piece of jagged concrete there as a reminder that God had saved me during the earthquake. I found and placed a second larger piece under the "survival stone." *Thank you for dying on the cross, forgiving my sins, and accepting me as your child.* I put a smaller stone on top of the stack. *Thank you for putting Christy, Josh, and Nathan in my life.* Another. *Thank you for helping us through Christy's depression.* I kept adding to my mini concrete memorial until I had a loose pile of ten or so stones.

Thank you for guiding my career and giving me opportunities to serve you and help others.

Thank you for being here with me now, and not abandoning me.

Collecting rocks in the elevator might have seemed silly to some, but thinking back to God's faithfulness in my life made a difference in my state of mind. It gave me courage, strength, and hope. At any time, I could reach over in the dark and grab a rock as a reminder that God was still working.

———

Evening eventually turned to night, and the chances of being rescued decreased. I guessed that it had been at least thirty hours since the earthquake, and I thought about how far I'd come and how far I had yet to go. During the initial quake, I had missed instant death by mere inches, yet I knew that each moment I lived after the quake only brought me closer to death.

If my life were a Hollywood movie, this was where my life should have flashed in front of my eyes. In a series of "fast cuts," scenes from my childhood, wedding day, and the birth of my boys would rapidly appear and disappear. But this wasn't a movie, and my past life never flashed in front of my eyes. I did, however, have glimpses of my future.

For a few hours during the night, as I relaxed with my eyes closed, I pictured my boys getting older. I saw us camping, hiking, fishing, and backpacking. I'd done most of these things with Josh, but I hadn't yet done them with Nathan. I watched them as they grew, and I saw myself attending sporting events and concerts. At their high school graduations, I was so proud as I watched them receive their diplomas. Then I was the one who enjoyed taking pictures of *their* children. They handed their babies to me, and I held them in my arms. I was a grandpa!

As these images washed over me, they seemed real, as if I was living them rather than imagining them. But I wasn't imagining the happiness; I could truly *feel* the joy, even in that elevator. As the visions faded from my mind, I felt like God had given me a gift — I saw myself in my boys' future. Though I didn't see this as proof that I was going to get out alive, it was still encouraging. *Thank you, God.*

19

THE FRENCH TEAM

Thursday Morning

Hotel Montana, Port-au-Prince

I spent most of the early hours of Thursday morning lying in the elevator, dozing on and off, but I didn't sleep much. I had become so tired that even during the waking moments my mind felt weak and somewhat dazed. I found my familiar enemy of discouragement creeping in to assault my mind. The assaults were harder to fend off with my weakened body. I reached out to my Jordan Basket and grabbed the rock I had placed there to thank God for being with me during this crisis. While I was truly grateful for the ways he had shown me I wasn't alone, I longed for an even deeper, more tangible experience of his presence.

Lord, in biblical times you sometimes sent angels to comfort your followers during times of deep distress, and sometimes you showed up physically yourself. I know I don't deserve it, but I'll ask anyway. Please send an angel. Please come to be with me physically. Comfort me in my time of distress.

No one could look at my situation and say I wasn't in a challenging position of almost biblical proportions. I was severely injured in a collapsed hotel, in a destroyed city, with no foreseeable way out. I needed God's wisdom, his assurance, and his presence. I needed his comfort. I felt that having God show up physically would instantly help me resolve all of my doubts and fears.

My biggest doubts still centered on whether or not God could take care of my family without me. Could he really be a father to my kids and a husband to my wife?

I asked again, not harshly, but urgently.

If you were here holding my hand, I don't think I would even have to ask these questions. They would just vanish.

———

During the night, Lukeson and I occasionally spoke to encourage each other. Jim and I did the same thing. Though none of us could see Thursday's dawning light, the increased sounds of helicopters passing over the hotel told us that morning was upon us.

We had made it through our second night. I hadn't slept much on Wednesday night, but I hadn't fought it either. It had been at least thirty-six hours since the earthquake, and my body seemed to be growing weaker at a much faster rate. I needed to save my remaining energy for my endgame plan. I wanted to find the balance between not waiting so long that I didn't have any strength left and executing a risky plan while there was still a chance of being rescued.

Despite the fact that the only person we'd made contact with — Sarla's outsider — hadn't come back, I still had hope for a rescue. More than any organization I'd ever been a part of, I knew Compassion valued life. I knew they would mobilize every resource they had to find me and any other missing staff. They would continue looking until all of us were found. But it wasn't just because we were on staff; they would do that for any child in their care who was missing. I also had confidence in Christy. Her passion and tenacity would ensure that no piece of rubble would go unturned if she could help it. Between Compassion and Christy, I had hope that rescuers were already looking for me by name.

But that hope was tempered because I wasn't sure if anyone knew where I was. Just days before leaving Colorado Springs, I had to change hotels. The original hotel where we planned to stay, the

Hotel Karibe, had lost our reservation. The Hotel Montana was more expensive but had rooms available. Ephraim had made my reservation, and no one in Compassion's U.S. office knew for sure where I was staying. Neither did Christy or any of my family. Unless Ephraim was safe and made contact with my office, no one knew I was here.

———

For the most part, things were quiet during the day on Thursday. I passed the time by listening to the adventures of Sarla. Earlier, Jim and the others decided it was pointless to have Sarla waiting by the hole she'd found. I agreed; whomever she spoke to wasn't coming back. The location she had described seemed so hidden and remote we wondered if anyone would see or hear her there again. So once more, Sarla painstakingly pushed herself in and out of spaces, looking for a better way to make contact with the outside world.

Jim and the others guided Sarla from room to room, encouraging her with their words to burrow through piles of debris, over ledges, and into new spaces when she was hesitant to move forward. She was the one taking risks for all of us, but they helped by talking her through each new decision she faced. I secretly wished she could be bolder and more aggressive, take more risks, and yell louder.

Easy for me to say! It wasn't like I was ready to pursue my risky endgame plan to secure our rescue.

During the day, Sarla worked her way into some type of garden or greenhouse. In addition to the debris from the building, she now found herself having to crawl over plants and broken pots. I wondered how much more of this she could take before she just gave up and stopped trying.

———

Lukeson and I spoke occasionally through the afternoon, but by Thursday evening, I could tell he wasn't doing well. He spoke less frequently and sounded exhausted. I tried my best to keep him encouraged and to pass on any news that might be positive.

"Sarla found a new room, and she's headed there now," I told Lukeson, passing on Jim's latest update.

"That's great, Dan-yell."

I knew it was hard for either of us to get excited when so little had happened, and our previous hope — the contact Sarla made with the outsider yesterday — turned out to be nothing. But trapped in our respective elevators, there was little we could do but wait to hear Jim's next update.

———

I could hear Jim and Sarla talking. When they finished, I asked what was happening.

"Sarla got herself near another opening to the outside. This one appears to be closer to the surface. She's yelling through it now."

"Help. Can you please help us?" Sarla's voice sounded weak. There was a pause, and then more conversation between Sarla and Jim.

His voice was excited as he filled me in. "She can see a tree and a beam of light from a helicopter. She can also hear voices."

Immediately, all of my senses were on alert. This was the most positive news we'd gotten since Sarla's first contact with the outside world over a day and a half ago.

"Jim, let's all yell again."

I told Lukeson what was happening, and when Jim counted off, we all started pounding on the walls and yelling "Help!" as loudly as we could. After repeating this a couple of times, we all got quiet, waiting to see if there was an answer.

I could hear Sarla yelling again in the distance, "Help, please! Can anyone help us?"

After another exchange with Jim, I learned that Sarla could hear voices. Only this time, instead of the sounds belonging to some distant crowd clamor, she could hear specific voices carrying on a conversation very close to her. In response, she hollered, trying to get their attention, but they failed to notice her.

"Can she scream any louder? Could she try a scream like one

you'd hear in a horror movie — high-pitched and without words?" I asked Jim. By now I was sitting up, tensed and ready to spring into action, except there wasn't anything I could do to help. So I stuck with offering feeble, unhelpful advice from my hole in the rubble.

Jim communicated with Sarla some more and then reported back. "She can see a person near her, but they can't hear her."

I was about ready to jump out of my skin. I felt like I was watching my favorite team try to score with only seconds left in the game. I could see the play developing, but I was helpless to execute it. So much was riding on this, and I wasn't content to just sit back and wait for it to happen, or, worse yet, fail to happen. I tried again. "What about throwing something through the hole? Or maybe waving something. Didn't she have a stick earlier?"

"Shhh, I think she's talking to someone. I'm trying to hear what they're saying."

"We're Americans; we're trapped, and we need help." I held my breath as she spoke. I could hear Sarla talking, but I couldn't make out much of what she was saying. After a few minutes of conversation, I heard Jim passing on information about Lukeson and me. *Was it possible?*

I didn't want to say anything to Lukeson until I knew for sure, so I waited impatiently for Jim to update me. Finally, the news came.

"Sarla made contact with a French rescue team! They've asked for all of our names and a summary of our injuries. They're promising to come right back as soon as they get the equipment they need to rescue us."

This was the best news we'd had since the earthquake hit. An actual rescue team! For the first time, I had real hope that I would be rescued. *I will see Christy and the boys again!* I pumped my fist and let out a whoop of happiness. Jim and the others started singing the Doxology, and I joined in:

> *Praise God, from whom all blessings flow;*
> *Praise him, all creatures here below;*
> *Praise him above, ye heavenly host;*
> *Praise Father, Son, and Holy Ghost. Amen.*

"Dan-yell, what's going on?"

In all of the excitement, I had forgotten to tell Lukeson what was happening. "Sarla made contact with French rescuers. We'll all be out of here soon!"

Lukeson's voice quivered as he spoke. "Dat's good. Very good news."

Only now did I realize how weak and tired he really was. "Hang in there, Lukeson; it's only a matter of hours now."

Over the next few minutes, Jim updated me on what had happened. Apparently, Sarla's yelling was heard by a rescuer who spoke French. He didn't understand what she was saying and couldn't see where her voice was coming from, so he brought over a second team member, who spoke some English. That time, when Sarla yelled, the rescuer understood.

Though the English-speaking rescuer could hear her, he still couldn't see where she was. Sarla tried to explain her location but couldn't communicate it clearly. Then she got the idea to stick her leg through the hole. When the rescuer saw it, he immediately rushed to the opening and spoke to her.

He asked for information on those who were trapped. Sarla gave him the names and conditions of the five who were trapped together and then asked Jim for information on Lukeson and me. She relayed all the information to the rescuer, who wrote it down on a list.

My name was on a list!

It's amazing how good it felt to know that rescuers had my name — that I was accounted for and on a list! No longer was I missing and unknown. Someone knew I was here, someone who could rescue me. Thanks to Sarla and her bravery, people would know where I was and, most importantly, that I was still alive!

While we waited for the rescuers to return, there was a lot of hopeful talk, but in the back of my mind, I couldn't help but wonder if this group too — like the outsider Sarla had talked to the day before — would fail to return. When I cautiously mentioned my concern to Jim, he immediately dismissed my fears with some encouraging news.

"I'm not sure how many are on the team," said Jim, "but at least one person is staying with Sarla and hasn't left."

This news reassured me greatly, and I updated Lukeson on the status. "One of the rescuers remained with Sarla, and the others will return shortly. We could be out of here in a few hours!"

"Dat's good, Dan-yell."

Though he continued to sound weak, this time I could hear joy in his voice.

———

An hour or two later, Jim updated me with the news we'd all been waiting for. "The team is back, and they've got equipment."

I couldn't contain my joy. This was really going to happen. *I'm going to be rescued!* Though I knew there was still a lot that needed to happen, I was so relieved that after all of my prayers and all of my concern for my family, I would have another chance to be with them. I imagined holding Christy in my arms, smelling her hair and kissing her soft, warm lips. I thought of the boys, and I pictured them squealing as they ran into my arms as I hugged and kissed them. Though they might not understand how close to death I had come, I knew that each and every time I looked at them from now on, I would remember how different it could have been. It was hard to believe I would actually return home, but I welcomed it and vowed that some things would be different moving forward.

Through Sarla, we learned the rescue would likely take a minimum of two hours. The French team would work to make the opening larger, layer by layer, so they could get into the hole where Sarla was and get her out — but also so they could bring equipment in to rescue the others who were trapped.

It was around 10:00 p.m. on Thursday night. I imagined that once they got in, it would take a couple more hours for them to get Jim and the others out. By my best guess, Lukeson and I would see the morning sun.

But not all of my thoughts were happy. I realized I would be returning to Colorado Springs without David. I thought of his family and wished the outcome would have been different.

"Lukeson, I don't speak French, so when the rescuers get here, will you please tell them to retrieve David's body?" It wasn't much, but I hoped that at least having closure would help his loved ones.

"OK," he said. His voice sounded even weaker than the last time we had spoken. Lukeson was fading fast. The rescuers couldn't get here soon enough.

———

Jim could communicate to the rescuers through Sarla, and I could speak with them through Jim. They started working around ten. I heard the loud knocking of the jackhammers first. The noise surprised me. I didn't expect rescuers to use equipment that would cause vibrations. I pictured them on top of piles of rubble, and the walls and debris beneath them shifting as they bore their way through several layers of concrete. I wondered how safe that was.

The zzzzzz of the concrete saws came next, and occasionally I could hear the sound of a drill. The noise and vibrations created a symphony of hope inside my chest. Occasionally, they would all stop working at the same time, and I could hear someone speaking with Sarla. My heart would stop briefly while I strained to listen, willing them to resume their work. When they got whatever information they were after, they continued with the sounds of rescue, and I could exhale again.

Around 10:45 the rescuers were in, and Sarla led them to Jim's group. With the availability of their lights, she no longer had to stumble around. She was able to guide them directly to his space. I wondered if they were walking or crawling, and I realized I had no mental image of the risky terrain that Sarla had braved for us. Jim also kept me posted on what was happening, though I could hear much of it myself. "It's about ten fifty, Dan. Sarla is out! The rescuers are here with us."

I couldn't make out exactly what was said, but it sounded as though it would take an hour or two to get Jim and his group out. That meant it would likely be three or four more hours for Lukeson and me.

This was real and it was happening! I was elated. Not only were the rescuers at the site and working, but they had already accomplished a rescue — Sarla had been freed, and I was on a list of future rescues. *Four more hours, and I could be out of here! Thank you, God!*

Rescue wasn't coming a moment too soon. I could hear the injured men who were with Jim, and it seemed as if their pain and discomfort were increasing. Their cries became more frequent. But there was also joyful singing. Between the rescuers, the equipment, and the voices from Jim's group, it was as if the entire area had exploded in sound.

———

Around midnight, the rescuers reached Jim and the others. Jim and Rick, one of the men trapped with Jim, were the first to go.

"Dan, they're freeing us. But they're still here working on Clint and Sam, whose legs are pinned. Ann is staying to translate for them, and we're leaving now."

"God bless you, Jim! I am so glad you're out!"

"They know about you and your Haitian friend. We'll remind them to come for you."

"Thanks, Jim!"

And then Jim was gone.

I was happy that he was out, but since he was the most communicative of those in his group, I knew I would miss his updates. Nonetheless, it was good news for all of us. I couldn't wait to tell Lukeson.

"Lukeson, Jim is out!"

There was no response.

"Lukeson, did you hear me? Jim is out. They got Jim and Rick out, and now they're working on the others."

Still no response. I banged on the wall.

"Lukeson, can you hear me?"

"Yes."

Maybe he had been sleeping, or maybe he was just so very weak. Either way, I wanted him to have hope to hold on to; the rescuers would come for us very soon.

20

CHOICES

Palm Sunday 1998

Monrovia, California

"Leave me alone!" Christy said, pushing the lock button on the car door. But she made the mistake of leaving the window down.

I leaned through the driver's window, reached across, and tried to grab the keys out of the ignition, but she beat me to it. She grabbed my arm with her left hand and then pulled the keys out of the ignition with her right, holding them out toward the passenger side so I couldn't reach them.

She was so upset, I was concerned she might harm herself. There was no way I was going to let her drive. "You're not leaving," I said, diving headfirst through the driver's side window. I wedged my body between her and the steering wheel so I could reach the keys and wrestle them out of her right hand. Fortunately, my arms were longer, and I was able to grab them. Unfortunately, when my right arm recoiled, I elbowed her in the nose.

"Ow!" she yelled.

"Sorry." I felt bad, and I was glad to see she wasn't bleeding. "But you're angry, and I'm not going to let you take the car."

I unlocked and opened the driver's door, forcing her to move. "Let me drive," she protested weakly, still holding her nose. But she had no choice. She climbed over the stick shift and into the passenger seat because I was getting in, whether she liked it or not. The passenger door was stuck closed because of damage from an accident, so Christy couldn't get out on her side of the car.

I started the car.

"What are you doing?" she asked as she flipped down the sun visor and opened the mirror to take a look at her nose.

"I thought you wanted to go for a drive." I put on my seat belt and started the car.

She slammed the visor up and put on her seat belt. "I did, but not with you."

"We're going together."

I looked over my shoulder and shifted into reverse. She slumped in her seat and turned her head to look out the window. We were five years into our marriage — five years into Christy's depression.

It was Palm Sunday, and it was a beautiful day. I headed toward the hills to a spot that overlooked Azusa and Glendora. We used to go there a lot when we were dating. We'd park and talk for hours. We needed to talk, and I couldn't think of a better spot.

———

As we drove through the foothills, I could see signs of spring. Plants were turning green, flowers were budding, and birds were singing. But I wasn't thinking about things that were fresh and new; I was thinking about things that were dying — Christy's faith, our marriage, and my hope.

Something had to change, and it had to change today.

I pulled the car into our usual spot, overlooking the valley below. I turned off the engine. Then I waited for her to speak.

"This isn't working. I want to give up."

I was past the optimistic encouragement I usually offered. Instead, I spoke the truth. "You're right. It isn't working. So what are we going to do about it?"

I was facing a crisis of faith. After years of frustration and disappointments, I felt very far from God. I didn't know how to talk to him, and I didn't know how to trust him. *God, what is going on? Did I miss something?*

"I've been thinking." Her brown eyes searched mine as she spoke. "Maybe I should just move home with my parents. I'm holding you back. If I go live with them, they can take care of me. You can divorce me and move past all this."

"Is that what you want?"

"I want to get better, but that's not happening. And I don't want to hurt you anymore." I could see the dejection in her eyes and watched the tears pooling before she wiped them away with her fingertips.

"Should we just give up then?"

"Yes." Her answer didn't surprise me. She'd been saying this more frequently over the past few months.

"OK," I said. "Maybe we should give up on everything."

I could see that my statement startled her. She turned and looked at me. This wasn't how this conversation normally went. Usually she wanted to give up, and I was the one who fought back. Now I was agreeing with her. But maybe her parents *could* do something for her that I couldn't. We were at the end. We had tried everything. Nothing was going to change unless we did something drastic.

"Maybe we should give up on God too." I looked out my window. "Why hasn't he intervened and ended this depression?"

A few months ago, I could not have imagined thinking something like this, let alone saying it out loud to Christy. But I was exhausted. I had been carrying both of us for so long, fighting for hope, fighting for faith. Trying to be loving, trying to be patient, and failing in so many ways. I didn't think I could fight the fight alone any longer.

"Are you serious?" she asked. I looked at her and saw the tears begin to trickle down her face.

"I am. I don't know what else to do." I wiped my own tears on the back of my hand and closed my eyes.

She cried quietly for a few minutes. I sat in awkward silence, not sure what to do or what to say. *Is this really what I want? Is there no other choice?*

Christy didn't speak.

She didn't have to.

I already knew she was feeling the same way. If *I* wasn't fighting for hope, who would? And as I took it all in, I started to weep. I buried my face in my hands and cried for Christy, for our failing marriage, and for the loss of a faith I once held so dear.

21

"WE'RE ON THE LIST!"

Thursday Night

Hotel Montana, Port-au-Prince

After Jim left, I knew I wouldn't get updates as frequently. So I strained to listen to and discern the sounds of rescue for myself. I heard a French woman's voice, and though I didn't speak French, from the conversation, she seemed to be the one in charge. The others referred to her as *Capitaine*. I assumed it was the word *captain* in French. She had a loud, clear voice, and it was easy to hear things she said, whether I could understand them or not.

At one point, I heard Capitaine reciting a list of our names. When she said "Dan Woolley," it sounded more like "Dan Jelly." I didn't care what they called me as long as they knew I was here. For the next few minutes, I heard the French rescuers talking among themselves. I assumed they were working on their plan.

"Dan, do you hear me?" It was Capitaine.

"Yes, I hear you!"

"OK, these last two rescues are taking a little longer than expected. We didn't forget about you. We know that you and your Haitian friend are in the elevators, and as soon as we're done here, you guys are next."

From what I could tell, the French team was working to pull out Clint and Sam, the ones with severe leg injuries. Because the rescue no longer involved the sounds of heavy equipment, it was difficult to hear what kind of progress was being made. I was thankful for her update. Based on the early reports, I had expected them to spend about two hours getting Jim and his friends out, but it had taken at least twice that long. I was worried about Lukeson, who had grown steadily weaker. *Could he hang on much longer?*

A few minutes after I had spoken with Capitaine, I heard what sounded like a shift change. New people came in, and Capitaine left. It sounded as if Ann, the woman who was trapped with Jim, left at that time also. While I could occasionally hear French voices, I no longer heard any English. I hoped they knew that Lukeson and I were still here and waiting.

———

It had been a long time since I last heard the rescuers' voices. I wasn't sure how much time had passed. Things had been quiet from Jim's old area for a while. I could only assume everyone was out.

Tools were being used in other parts of the building. I could hear the pulsating jackhammers and the sounds of the saws in the distance off to my right. But Jim's area, to my left and slightly below me, was silent. I assumed that's where the French team would come from. So I waited patiently to hear the same sounds of rescue coming from there.

I had no way to know for sure what was between my area and Jim's former space. But in my mind, I pictured one or two concrete walls separating us, plus the ceiling that had fallen and cut my head. In my simplistic view of the situation, I envisioned rescuers making four cuts in each wall — left side, top, right side, bottom — and then pulling or pushing a square of concrete out of the way so they could get to the next area. If they hadn't reached me yet, if there were more walls in the way, they would just repeat the process.

I figured that if they did this two or three times — somewhere between eight and twelve cuts — they'd pop out into the lobby in front of our elevators. Of course, there was a chance it might not be that clean. Perhaps they'd have to prop up a beam or two to keep things from falling. But still, I imagined it should only take them an hour or two to reach me once they got started. Then they'd pry Lukeson's door open and get him out, and we'd both be free. I waited to hear the sounds of the concrete saws.

———

The equipment remained silent. Maybe they're regrouping. I realized it might be more complicated than I thought. Maybe they were taking time to figure out a rescue plan that would keep everyone safe.

More time passed.

Perhaps they needed a break? I knew the work had to be hot, dusty, and tiring. They must have stopped to drink water or get something to eat. It was the middle of the night. If they had been working on other rescues all day, of course they needed to eat, or perhaps even take a short rest. They should start up again in an hour or so.

———

Still more time passed. Were they getting new equipment and tools?

I was running out of excuses. They had led me to believe they would work through the night to get me out, but it seemed like hours since I had heard any sounds of rescue. The French team knew I was still here; my name was on the list, right? *Maybe they got distracted and forgot about us.* I decided to pound on the elevator wall to get the attention of rescuers working in other parts of the building. I wanted to remind everyone that Lukeson and I were still in the elevators.

I picked up a piece of concrete, knocked it against the wall, and yelled, "Helllp!" I repeated this several times, and then stopped to listen. I was hoping to hear the voice of Capitaine. I wanted to hear her say, "We're still here, and we'll get you out soon." But I heard nothing.

When the French team had first connected with Sarla, they had done a great job of staying constantly connected with us, updating us about what they were doing and what to expect. During and after

Jim's rescue, Capitaine had kept me informed directly, but since the shift change there had been nothing.

Have they forgotten me?

I repeated the banging and yelling. This time I heard Lukeson join in. I was glad to hear him; I hoped resting had helped him to rally. We continued banging for a period of time. Then we stopped, and I listened carefully. Still no response. My anxiety level was rising.

Every two or three minutes, I picked up my concrete brick and banged. I couldn't yell every time; it took too much energy, but when I did, I yelled as loudly as I could. But the weaker I got, the less sound I made. Trying to be more intentional, I thumped the wall as rhythmically as possible. Tap-tap. Pause. Tap, tap, tap. I didn't want it to sound like random noise; I wanted anyone who was listening to know it was intentional.

After we banged, I always stopped to listen. Occasionally, I could make out bits and pieces of conversations. I could hear what sounded like crew leaders calling out instructions to their teams, but it seemed that they couldn't hear me.

The banging was wearing both of us out. We stopped doing it every two or three minutes, waiting twice as long between each session. We occasionally yelled, "There are two of us, and we're in the elevators." At some point, we stopped out of pure exhaustion. That's when I heard an American rescuer — I assumed a team captain — say, "I've got two new contacts here. My crew can't get to them. I need a new crew!"

His words scared and angered me. *New contacts?* Immediately, I yelled back, "We're not new. We're on the list!" I paused, but no one acknowledged that they'd heard me. "We're on the list! Don't forget us." I continued alternating between yelling and listening, but I could hear no response.

I thought about what was going on aboveground. Who was in charge up there? Would this captain be able to get another crew? Did they have the list? Did they know we were still down here?

From the sounds of tools and equipment around me, I could tell there were several crews each doing their own thing. That's when it struck me — I could be forgotten in the chaos. My heart nearly stopped as my concern grew. *They didn't pass on the list to the new shift. They don't know we're here!* Could they have mixed Lukeson and me up with other survivors? Could they have rescued someone else and thought they'd gotten us?

I'd always known that my only hope of rescue was from someone on the outside. But it never occurred to me that once they showed up, I wouldn't be able to rely on them to get me out. With so many teams working around the hotel, I wondered what systems they had in place to make sure they kept track of everybody.

In addition, with all of the commotion, I had to wonder what kinds of choices the rescuers were forced to make. If other survivors were easier to get to, would they rescue them first?

My initial hope of being rescued after the earthquake had been nothing more than mere embers. But during the past few hours, those embers had been fanned with the hope of rescue, and they burned brightly. Now though, as I considered the chaos that must exist outside the rubble pile — multiple teams, languages, and command structures — I realized that my recent hope had been extinguished. Being forgotten was a very real possibility.

Unfortunately, I was more vulnerable now than I'd ever been. Though rescuers were all around me, without the help of Jim and Sarla to connect me to the outside world, there was no way for them to know I was here. I was in the middle of the building, buried at the bottom of six stories of concrete, and in the most remote part of what was left of the Hotel Montana. No one would look for survivors here.

Once again, I started thinking that death was a likely outcome. But facing death now was harder, because I had glimpsed so much hope of being rescued.

My breaths came more quickly and were shallower. *I can't hyperventilate now!* I felt adrenaline racing through my veins, and anger was seething right behind it.

The thought of dying because someone forgot to pass on a list with my name on it was killing me. I realized it was up to me to make sure the rescuers knew I was here. Until now, I had shared the responsibility of yelling for attention with the others — it had been a team effort. And while Lukeson would go along with whatever I asked, he wasn't initiating. It would be up to me to let the outside world know we were here.

For several minutes, I banged and yelled almost constantly. I only stopped long enough to listen for a response. After a while, I had to lie down and rest because I was so physically worn-out.

As I lay on the elevator floor panting, dust clogged my nose and covered my lips. I began to despair. I didn't want to waste the battery of my iPhone, but I turned it on quickly to check the time.

It was three fifteen in the morning.

Sarla was the first one taken out around eleven o'clock last night. Ann was the last to leave around one o'clock this morning.

It had now been eight hours since the first rescuers showed up, and at least two and a half hours since the last contact with the French team.

If I wasn't sure before, I knew it now.

The rescuers weren't coming back.

22

WORSHIP TIME

I am going to die because someone lost a list.

I picked up the concrete brick and banged and yelled. It was a healthy way of taking out my anger and frustration. I wasn't going to accept my elevator death sentence just because of someone's communication error!

———

More time had passed, and I debated my endgame plan again, but there were still problems with it. Even if I could figure out how to use the iPhone as a light source, even if I could boost myself up and into the elevator shaft, and even if I could climb the shaft without falling, how would I force open the elevator doors on the floors above me? At a minimum, I would need a crowbar.

I probably should have been worried about how weak I was becoming. Instead, I just lay on the floor panting and trying to come up with a plan for what to do next.

OK, God. If I am going to die here, so be it. But I'm still worried about my family. And I don't understand how you can bring good for my family in spite of my death.

I had expended an inordinate amount of energy banging and yelling, yet it was the diminishing of hope that drained all of my strength. Almost being rescued and then realizing it wasn't going to happen was worse than never thinking I'd be rescued at all.

151

While the buzz from the saw blades and drill bits continued in the distance, they didn't seem to be getting any closer to me. I could no longer hear voices, and there was no further sound of the American captain who had asked for a new team to rescue survivors he'd identified.

It would be so easy to just close my eyes and die right here. But I fought the urge. *The rescuers are very near; they'll get to us eventually. Just hang on until they get here.* Still, I began to suspect it could be a matter of days, not hours, before they got to me. It was also possible that the tools being used could unsettle something and send the remaining walls crashing down.

I wondered about the instructions given to the rescue teams. Were they told, like the Marines, to get everyone out and not leave anyone behind? Or were they like some civilian teams that were told just to rescue and treat those they could safely save? I hoped it was more of a Marine mentality out there, but I could understand why in a situation where so many people needed to be rescued, it would be smart to cherry-pick the easy ones first. If there were fifty kids in a schoolroom somewhere across Port-au-Prince, it made more sense to take people and equipment there and rescue as many of them as possible. And I hoped they would make that choice, but where would that leave me?

I wasn't sure if it mattered what their plan was. Even if they desired to get me out, I didn't know if they could. Obviously, the captain of the American team couldn't get a crew when he needed one, and the French team had made promises and then disappeared. Just because someone was a member of a rescue team, or even a captain of that team, it didn't mean they had full control over who would get rescued and who wouldn't. I resigned myself to spending several more days in my elevator.

As I thought about spending additional time trapped, I grew more concerned about dehydration. I could feel myself getting weaker. While I could probably go without food for several more days, I knew I couldn't live as long without water.

My backpack! I had two bottles of water, one attached to each side. If I could find the pack, I would have enough water to last a few more days.

The aftershocks seemed to be over, and the walls and debris outside the elevator hadn't shifted since the first aftershock. Though I wasn't willing to risk it before, it now seemed worth the risk to venture outside of the elevator to search for my backpack in the lobby. It couldn't be far from where I was when it was knocked from my back as the quake hit.

I didn't have much to lose — I was already feeling pretty frail — and I had everything to gain. I pulled myself up with the handrail. I noticed how much weaker I was. It took both arms to pull myself up, and then I had to steady myself before I could take a couple of feeble steps.

I had become familiar with the dark confines of my elevator, but venturing outside the shaft would be dangerous because I didn't know what was out there. I decided to use my iPhone for light. I knew there was another battery extender inside the pack; if I could find the pack, I'd have more battery power.

I moved cautiously, groping with my hands and using the light sparingly. I didn't see the backpack anywhere. I flashed the phone in the general direction of where I'd seen David's leg in my picture, knowing this was where I had been too. I cautiously took steps toward the wall, being careful not to step on ... *That's not David's leg!*

Instead, it was a board covered in blood. That's *my* blood! I must have crawled across it on my way to the elevator. I stared, surprised at the amount of blood. I had thought that was David's leg when I saw it in the picture. I had cried about that leg, and now I could see it was just a board. Relief swept over me.

I didn't want to stay in the lobby any longer than I had to, so I took another quick look around, but I didn't see my backpack or any signs of David. I noticed a futon couch covered in a tropical print. I tried to grab the large cushion, but when I couldn't get it to budge, I settled for one of the dusty pillows and grabbed it to take back to the elevator. Though my attempt to find my backpack was a failure, at least the pillow would bring a nice bit of comfort.

I hobbled back to the elevator. By the time I lay back down, I was breathing heavily. I thought about the blood smeared on the board and had a new appreciation for how severe my leg wound was.

Knowing it wasn't David's leg also lightened my mood. Though it had been two and a half days, and I hadn't heard a sound from him, at least I was no longer *positive* that he was dead. There was still hope.

"Lukeson, are you there?"

"Yes, Dan-yell." His voice wavered.

"I just walked around the lobby to see if I could find water. Remember how I told you my friend David had died?"

"Yes."

"Well, what I thought was his leg, wasn't. There's still a chance he may be alive."

"Oh."

"Listen, Lukeson, if the French rescuers come back and I'm not here, will you please tell them to look for David?"

I didn't have to explain what I meant about not being here. Lukeson would know, because he also felt death's breath on the back of his neck.

"Yes."

"Thanks."

I could tell he didn't have the energy to talk more, which was fine, because I didn't either. Since I couldn't find the water, I tried to think about what other sources I had for sustenance. I considered eating paper from my journal, but I realized there wouldn't be any nutritional value in that. *I wonder if my passport cover is made of leather.* Even if it wasn't, I wondered if putting something — anything — in my stomach would ease the hunger pains that had been intensifying. I kept the option open and did the only thing I could physically do here in the elevator: I prayed.

Father, I so want to believe that you can bring good out of any situation and even bring good to my family if I die. But I just can't

*see it. I can't imagine how anything other than rescuing me would be
a good plan for them. Please intervene!*

*I'm not going to bargain with you, God. I'm not going to say, "If
you do this, I'll do that." But you tell us to bring our requests to you.
So I'm going to tell you again what I want. Father, I want to go back
to my family. And you can do it. You have the power to get me out
of here safely. You saved Daniel from the lions' den, and his friends
from the fiery furnace. You've already performed miracles to keep me
alive. There are rescuers all around me, so please, God, please rescue
me!*

Despite the moments of encouragement and peace I had experienced from God earlier in the elevator, I felt no peace now. I felt
nothing but worry and despair. Since the earthquake, I had oscillated
back and forth between fear of death and hope for rescue. And I had
processed both realities through my mind. Here in my weakened
condition, death seemed more likely than ever, and I felt all the worried moments I had experienced since the earthquake stacking on top
of me like the stories of this collapsed hotel.

I started shaking. My heartbeat echoed in my ears, and I could
hear my heart rate increasing. My breathing grew faster and shallower, and I tried to slow it down so I wouldn't hyperventilate. *Don't
panic!* Sweat soaked my T-shirt. I felt like I was losing control of my
body — as if it was rapidly breaking down and there was nothing I
could do to stop it. I felt despair unlike anything I had ever experienced before.

Once again, I heard God's calming voice in my mind: "*Worship
me.*"

Right now? Really? Typically I worshiped through prayer and
song, but I didn't feel like I could do either right now. But I decided
to try. While I wasn't ready to trust God for everything, I could trust
him with this request.

I closed my eyes and started singing "Arise, My Soul, Arise." As
I sang the words "my name is written on His hands," I choked up,
remembering that even if the French team lost their list of survivors,
God knew I was here — I was on *his* list. As I transitioned to "Be

Still, My Soul," I began to feel my body and spirit calm down. I sang the first verse, "Leave to thy God to order and provide; in every change, He faithful will remain." Intellectually I wanted to leave it all to God — to completely give him my situation and my fears. But I couldn't make my heart do it yet. I wasn't ready to accept the idea that, whether I lived or died, he would always take care of my family.

Verse, chorus, verse — I continued to sing other worship songs.

My heart rate returned to normal, and my sense of dread subsided. I lay on my back with my legs up on the opposite wall. While I was singing, I began to picture myself in a big field, as if I were in the middle of someone's farm. Above me, a canopy of blinking stars shone brilliantly in the dark and clear night sky. As they danced and twinkled, I was their audience. Nothing obstructed my vision.

I marveled at the view. It wasn't a picture, and the scene wasn't static. I saw wispy clouds floating below the stars. And I wasn't just watching the scene; I was in it. I even felt a light breeze on my skin. All of the debris had made it musty in the elevator, and I hadn't felt the air stir at all. Yet lying there watching the clouds in motion, I could feel the breeze that moved them. I felt as if I had been transported. No longer was I lying in the elevator; instead, I was sitting in a shallow pool of warm water or perhaps a Jacuzzi. I even felt like I could dip my fingers in the water and they would get wet.

It all felt so real that I wondered if I was hallucinating. I opened my eyes, and the whole scene went away — I found myself back in the complete darkness of my elevator. I closed my eyes and returned to the vision. It was a bit like waking up and then closing my eyes and returning to a dream, but I was fully conscious and in control the whole time.

In college, someone asked, "What part of nature connects you to God?" For me, it was always the same: ocean waves, stars, and a breeze ruffling the trees on a mountain. They were symbols of his power, and in their presence it was easy to believe that God's Spirit still moves on the earth, still moves in our lives. If I had to pick the most peaceful place I could imagine, the one place where I felt most bathed in God's love, it would be an open field under the stars. That's what I was experiencing.

My college roommate had written one of my favorite worship choruses, setting Psalm 40 to music. The words really spoke to me as I sang them.

> *I waited patiently for the Lord;*
> *he inclined his ear and heard my cry.*
> *He lifted me from the pit,*
> *out of the mud and mire;*
> *he set me on a rock.*
> *He put a new song in my mouth,*
> *a hymn of praise to our God.*

I closed my eyes as I sang, and I made the words my prayer. I knew God had heard my cry — when I asked for his presence and comfort, he had responded. This worship experience was lifting me from my pit at the bottom of the hotel and transporting me onto unshakable ground, where I could sit in perfect peace and absolute security.

The singing continued, and one song flowed into another, as if there was a divine worship leader and I was just following along. I felt the wind on my face and the water gently warming my body.

Tears rolled down my face — tears of joy. I could feel God's presence more intimately than I ever had in my life. He was with me, just like I had asked. He wasn't just the audience in this worship experience, but somehow he was a participant in a two-way dialogue. As I sang, my spirit spoke with him about my worries; my hopes for my life, my family; my gratefulness for his grace and his sacrifice on the cross. I heard from him words of encouragement, reminders of his power and his love for me — even his delight in me.

Although I couldn't see his face or hold his hand, I felt as though he had graced me with his presence. He was here with me in an intimate and powerful way during my dying hours. I couldn't tell how long this worship experience continued. Maybe a half hour, maybe hours — the experience transcended time.

Eventually, the worship time came to an end, and, reluctantly, I let the vision slip away. As I lay overwhelmed and worn-out — yet still in the afterglow of the experience — I was aware of a clear and unmistakable message from God. This time it was not like I was hearing specific words in my mind, but rather like I was hearing the final note of our worship time, like the sustained resonance that lingers in the air after the ringing of a bell.

Trust me, with everything.

And so, finally, I did. I trusted God with my crisis. I trusted him with my death. I trusted him with my family after I died — with Christy, with Josh, and with Nathan. My questions were resolved. My fears were gone. It's not that I *understood* how God would make something good from my death, but I knew that, because of his power and love, he would. The majesty and awesome beauty that I had just witnessed and the love and grace that he had poured on me in such a personal way were evidence enough. My Father would make this situation work out for the good. Guaranteed.

He would be a father to Josh and Nathan and a husband to Christy. He would make my life and my death matter in their lives, and his good purposes would be fulfilled. Somehow there would be good through David's death as well, and God would care for his family in special ways. Even for the people of Haiti, who had to be suffering so much, God would bring good through the tragedy of this earthquake.

Thank you, Father, for showing me you can be trusted completely! I trust you. Let your will be done in this situation — whatever that may be.

My thoughts were interrupted by a voice from above.

"Hello. Is anybody there?"

23

HEARING VOICES

Though it was startling, I knew the voice was real and not a figment of my imagination. "Yes! Yes! I'm here. I'm here!" I yelled. "Can you hear me?"

"Yes, I can hear you. What's your name?"

"Dan. Dan Woolley, and I'm trapped in the elevator. My Haitian friend, Lukeson, is in the elevator next to me."

"OK, Dan. My name is Sam, and I'm in the elevator shaft above you. Can you see my light?"

"No, I can't."

"That's OK. I'm going to try and come down through the shaft, but I have to go back up first and grab some equipment, then I'll be right back."

He'll be right back? What did he mean by he'll be right back?

This wasn't the American captain I'd talked to a while ago; this was *another* new guy. He was talking to me as if he'd never heard of me, like he hadn't seen the list either.

What did this mean? I'd already had two captains, one American and one French, who promised to get me out. They'd both failed to come back. What if a superior didn't let Sam come back? What if he got pulled out to do another job? I had gotten my hopes up too many times in the past hours only to be left hoping and waiting for people who didn't come back.

Whoever Sam was, he'd just confirmed my suspicion that there were communication difficulties because of the chaos. I wondered how many teams there were and how many countries were represented, and whether anyone was in charge. The peace I had felt moments ago disappeared quickly, and I felt the panic start to rise again.

Lukeson must have been sleeping during my worship time, because I hadn't heard anything from him, but when I started pounding on the elevator walls, he woke up and joined me by pounding and yelling.

People were working in different parts of the building now, and I could hear their voices, but I didn't know if they heard mine. I would bang and yell, then stop to listen. That's when I heard the sound of yet another American. This was at least the third. His voice seemed to come from the place where Jim used to be.

I yelled in his direction. "Hey, we're in the elevator. There are two of us trapped in the elevators!"

He heard me.

"We got a guy over here." I heard him call to his teammates. Then he yelled back to me, "We're going to try to get you out."

I wasn't sure that was exactly what he said, because the sound of his voice was drowned out by equipment sounds coming from another rescue team in the distance.

I heard the buzzing of the concrete saw from Jim's former area, indicating that the rescuers were indeed working their way toward me. I tried to count the number of cuts: One. Two. A pause. Three. Four. And then a longer pause. This fit with my earlier assumption that there would probably be four cuts and then a pause as they pushed the piece through the wall to see if I was there.

The pattern repeated. Then again.

I was encouraged. The sounds were making sense; they were coming for me.

Then there was another long pause followed by a new pattern. *How many cuts do they have to make to get to me?*

The sounds weren't synching with the pictures in my mind.

Surely, there weren't that many walls between where Jim had been and where I was now. It was taking too long. Something was wrong.

When the saws paused, I yelled again.

"Hey, I'm still here! I'm in the elevator." Sometimes my cries were to help them identify my location, but mostly they were my way of making sure they didn't forget us.

The saws ceased.

An American captain joined the man who sounded closest to me. The walls separating us dampened their voices, so I could only make out portions of the conversation.

"What are you doing?"

"I'm working toward the guys in the elevator."

The captain's reply vaguely sounded like, "How many men you got working on that?"

"Bftoo."

Though I couldn't understand the man's muffled answer, the captain's response was very clear. "We can't afford to spend our time on that right now. Our shift's almost over."

There was another muffled statement from my rescuer, followed by the sound of a drill starting up again. "You're on your own time then," the captain shouted angrily over the noise of the tools.

Did he really just say that? What did that mean?

With horror, I realized that even if the rescuer knew I was here, apparently his ability to save me was based on the directions from his captain. If his shift ended, if he were hurt, or if he stopped for a break, there was no guarantee anyone else would ever know where I was.

I no longer believed anyone knew my name or knew I was trapped in the elevator. I couldn't trust the rescue crews.

It became clear that if I was going to be rescued, it was up to me to let them know I was here. Even if there was one lowly guy out there, and even if he was working against the wishes of his captain, I wanted to make sure he heard me. So every few minutes, I used chunks of concrete to bang against the metal side of the elevator. "Don't forget us!" I yelled. Or, "We're here!" I banged and screamed until I was exhausted. Then I'd rest and repeat. I had to make sure he knew I was here, make sure I wasn't forgotten again.

Then the drilling stopped.

I couldn't hear anything. *Why isn't he continuing?* I tried to make sense of what happened. *Did the captain tell him to stop? Did the rescuer decide he didn't want to work on his own time? Did he leave to go talk to his captain?*

I could hear jackhammers in the distance.

The sound of saws from above.

Voices to my left.

They spoke French.

And English.

And other languages I couldn't recognize.

It was getting harder to keep track of where the sounds were coming from. The clamor of the tools and the voices mixed and separated like two tracks on a stereo with a failing speaker.

I was feeling more desperate, and I started screaming, "We have injuries. We're injured."

My throat constricted, and my chest tightened. Short, shallow breaths made my heart race as I gasped for oxygen. For the first time since the quake hit, I succumbed to full-blown panic.

I was confused. I was trapped in the moment and could no longer remember things that had happened even a few minutes ago. I started to lose it.

Father, I accept your will in this situation, even if it means my death. But the rescuers are right here! Please don't abandon me when rescue is so close, so possible. If I'm going to die here, please let it happen quickly, not drawn out with rescuers and snatches of hope all around me.

I could hear the rescuers continuing to talk among themselves. My voice was noticeably weaker, but the panic increased my boldness, and I hollered, "Hey, we're in the elevator shaft. Help us! We're injured! There are two of us in the elevators. Can you hear me?"

"Quiet!"

I held my breath as the sounds ceased. *Had he heard me?* An

American was speaking, but I couldn't make out what he was saying. So I repeated myself, yelling at the top of my lungs, "There are two of us. We're in the elevators. We're injured!"

I could hear the voice clearly, as if the rescuer was right next to me. "We can't get to you," came the harsh reply.

Then the team started talking about other rescues they were working on. I could hear them discussing the specific details of their equipment. They sounded so close that it was like they were in the elevator with me.

"We need another saw in here."

"I need to change this bit."

It was as if they didn't know I was so close. Why can't they hear me? I let loose with everything I had. "We're right here! In the elevators!"

But their conversations continued without any acknowledgment they had heard me.

"Do you hear me? Do you hear me? Are you listening?" Lukeson joined my desperate cries for help, calling out in French, Creole, and other languages I didn't understand. I repeated his phrases, doing my best to imitate languages I didn't speak.

I heard an American voice. "We can't work on this guy."

Then I heard a French voice. I tried to get the French man's attention. "Don't forget us! Are you going to leave us? You can't leave us!"

"Be quiet! Be quiet!" someone yelled.

But I wouldn't shut up. I kept yelling.

Physically, I was growing weaker. I had the sense that my body was descending, like the feeling you get when you're almost asleep and you feel as though you're falling, but I wouldn't stop yelling and banging. The rescuers were as close as they'd ever been and I would do whatever it took to make them hear me.

To *make* them respond to me.

And then finally, one did.

"We're not coming for you. We're not going to rescue you! Shut up!"

24

I'M IN HELL

It was as if a blender had mixed the sounds of saw blades, drill bits, jackhammers, and voices into some sort of backward-playing, record-scratching audio mix. All I could hear was the slow motion recording of, "We're not coming for you. We're not going to rescue you! Shut up!"

"Hey, we're coming for you. I hear you," a rescuer said a few minutes later.

"You're coming for us?" I was surprised at the sudden turn of events. "We're here," I said. "We're here in the elevator." He sounded like he was right next to me.

I listened as he left his post to go and talk with his supervisor. "We can't go after just two," said his supervisor. "We can't dedicate all these resources to just two. You need to stop working."

So the rescuer stopped.

I could hear rescuers working in other parts of the building, but they weren't making progress toward Lukeson and me. "Do you hear us? Are you coming for us? Don't forget us!" I cried out.

"There's someone down there!"

It was another new voice, but as soon as he got interested in helping us, someone else spoke up. "Forget those two. Let's concentrate over here."

There were rescue groups from the United States, France, and other countries. Though they were working in different parts of the building, and each spoke their own language, I could still hear their conversations and understand every word they said, even when I didn't speak their languages.

They were taunting and teasing me with the hope of a rescue. They'd promise to come, but then they'd leave and go to work elsewhere. *Why are they doing this to me?* I couldn't imagine a worse torture.

God, are you still here with me? Are you? Why are you not rescuing me? If I'm going to die here, let me die quickly, not with this torturous hope of rescue all around me.

Then I had another thought.

Maybe he's not going to rescue me. Maybe God has left too.

The sense that I was physically descending continued. I yelled again.

"Shut up!" came the reply.

The words echoed inside my head, and I tried to make sense of them. Even in my disturbed state of mind, I knew no rescuer would ever say such a thing. I was convinced it couldn't be real. But if it wasn't real, why were the conversations continuing?

I was confused. It felt as though I was having flashes of hope followed by hours of despair. Darkness was all I'd known in the elevator, but now I felt a thick blanket of blackness covering my mind like a shroud, trying to snuff out all rational thought. Hope lay in a million broken pieces of concrete like a lightbulb that shattered after being tossed to the floor.

I couldn't see the walls because of the darkness, but I sensed they were gone. In front of me, I saw rescuers with tools, and they were digging, cutting, and sawing, but they couldn't see me. When they spoke, it sounded as if they were right next to me.

My heart raced. I couldn't make any sense of where I was or what was happening to me.

Voices blending in my head.

Whispering in my ear.

My throat constricted again, and my chest tightened.

It was getting harder to breathe, and I choked on the darkness.

And then suddenly … I knew.

I was *dead.*

I had died and gone to hell. I knew I was in hell because I was being tortured and God was no longer with me. He had abandoned me completely. The rescuers I saw and heard weren't real; they were visions sent to afflict me.

Hell was a place where heroin dangled before desperate addicts but was snatched away by an angry dealer before their trembling hands could grasp it. My drug of choice in this place was hope. While I caught an occasional glimpse of it, it was seized away before my mind could possess it.

It was sparkler hope that burned brightly and then fizzled to ashes. I was in hell holding the burned-out stick with the charred tip. The cruel torment was worse than any physical pain I'd ever felt.

Obviously, I was wrong about God accepting me. I was wrong about his grace. My heart was not right, and he did not forgive me.

That means all my prayers will go unanswered. My family will suffer, and God will not help them.

But why was Lukeson here? I understood if God didn't think *my* repentance was real. I had turned away from him a lot in my life, but my Haitian friend was sincere in his prayer. He didn't deserve this. I had thought I'd brought him to the gates of heaven; instead, we were together in the pits of hell.

My head pounded, and sweat dripped down my back. This experience of hell was more evil than I had ever imagined it to be. And now — it would be my home for eternity. I couldn't help but grieve for myself, for Lukeson, and, most of all, for my family.

There was no salve for the searing pain I felt, knowing my family was left to suffer without hope. If God ignored my prayers, then he would surely ignore theirs too. This was the worst possible scenario for Christy and the boys — I was in hell, and God was not going to take care of any of us.

I abandoned the idea of being rescued. If I am in hell, then I am in hell. There was no point in banging or yelling. *Why should I participate in this charade?*

I rolled onto my stomach and grasped the edge of the elevator car. I half dragged myself, half crawled out of the elevator. As I slid along the floor, I could feel my chest burning from being scratched and cut by concrete shards and rubble. I welcomed the pain; it felt better than the flames of despair that licked at my mind. Halfway out of the elevator, I slowly turned over so my back was lying on pieces of glass and concrete covering the floor. *What did it matter? I was in hell.*

There in the darkness, I searched for the face of my Accuser. But before I could look the Evil One in the eye, I heard a familiar voice.

"Dan. Dan! Can you hear me?"

25

BELIEVING

Palm Sunday 1998

Monrovia, California

"Dan. Dan! Can you hear me?"

It was Christy. "I said I think we should give God another chance."

I was stunned. Her comment caught me off guard.

"This time, we need to choose to trust him all the way and not hold things back."

"But we have been trying to trust him, haven't we?" I asked.

"Yes, we have. But I think there are things we've stopped trusting him with. We stopped going to church when it felt too hard. Maybe we should try again, and pray that God will help us find a church that will be more supportive in our pain. We haven't prayed or studied the Bible together for a long time. I'm willing to give it another try. How about you?"

I stared at her, not knowing what to say. It was like the old Christy was waking up a little. "Why the change?" I asked.

"I guess I'm not ready to completely give up yet."

She reached for my hand. I gently stroked the top of her hand with my thumb. I realized how significant it was to me that this was Christy's idea, not mine.

This turn of events wasn't an accident. It didn't just happen. God was speaking to Christy, and she was responding. Therefore he was also speaking to me through Christy. God was showing us that he hadn't abandoned or forgotten about us. At this crisis point of our lives, though I had been ready to abandon him, God was still with us.

———

The next Sunday was Easter, and we went to church. It took us a few months of searching to find a church where we felt comfortable — churches were still not the easiest places to bring our broken selves — but once we did, we started investing ourselves and even became involved socially. It wasn't easy, especially for Christy, but we did it. And things began to change.

Ironically, it seems that God used my moment of weakness on that Palm Sunday when I was ready to give up to help Christy access an inner strength she no longer believed she had. Her will to fight and survive came alive again. But there were no instant miracles. Christy continued to struggle with her depression for a while. That Palm Sunday was a turning point, but there were other factors that made a difference.

The conversations we had about past hurts, though tedious at times, really did pay off, and Christy began to experience some relief from pent-up pain. Over time, I learned more patience and sensitivity, and Christy discovered healthy ways to handle the disappointments and challenges that life brings. As we opened up to receive more help from others, Christy's parents got more involved, and their support of prayer, listening, and unconditional love was a significant help.

I don't think I'll ever understand why God sometimes feels the most silent, the most distant, at times when we need him the most. But looking back, I can see signs that God never left us, even in the darkest times, and he used this trial to grow our faith and establish in us a hunger for his presence.

As time passed, we noticed many things getting easier, and the hard things happened less often. We started going out on dates and picnics more often and meeting friends for dinner. We began to enjoy life again.

―――

There were candles on the table, and Christy had made a special dinner. I gazed into her eyes, happy to see them sparkling once again, and thought about how deeply I loved this woman.

"Happy sixth anniversary, Sweet. Here's to fifty more!" I said raising my glass. "I love you." It had been fourteen months since that momentous Palm Sunday when we started turning the corner on her depression.

"I love you too," she said meeting my glass with hers, causing a soft clink. "Would you still marry me, knowing what we went through to get to this anniversary?"

I looked deep into her brown eyes and didn't hesitate with my answer. "Absolutely! I would do it *all* over again just to be with you. And you're still as cute as the day I married you!"

"Cute?" she said batting her eyelashes at me in mock anger. "Did you say *cute*?"

"Yes I did. Why, what's wrong with that?"

"Well, last week you said I was *beautiful*." Her smile filled her face. Her whole body seemed to glow, and it wasn't from the candles.

"It's possible to be both, you know," I said, winking at her.

That's when I realized I no longer had to try to remember the last time Christy smiled; now it was an everyday occurrence.

―――

I sat on a hard plastic chair, absentmindedly playing with my wedding ring, twisting it back and forth while I waited for the oil in our car to be changed.

My tendency when facing adversity had always been to try to tough it out — to rely on my mind, my tenacity, and my strength of will to get me through difficult situations. But Christy's depression proved to be far beyond my capability to handle on my own, and I cried out to God like never before.

As Christy became healthier, she earned her master's degree in educational therapy and then worked with kids, helping them to overcome the challenges of learning disabilities. She knew something about persistence and fighting against challenges in your own brain, and she used her knowledge to help them succeed academically. In time, we started a family and began living the future we had hoped for.

As I looked at my wedding ring, I remembered how we had designed it specifically with Ecclesiastes 4:9–12 in mind. Those verses read:

> Two are better than one,
>   because they have a good return for their work:
> If one falls down,
>   his friend can help him up.
> But pity the man who falls
>   and has no one to help him up!
> Also, if two lie down together, they will keep warm.
>   But how can one keep warm alone?
> Though one may be overpowered,
>   two can defend themselves.
> A cord of three strands is not quickly broken.

A cord of three strands really has described our faith and our relationship through the years. I thought about how I'd spent years pulling Christy up. But when we were at the end of our rope, she was the one who hung on, and God showed that his strength was working in us all along.

He was our firm foundation and the strand that bound us together. I had every reason to believe he always would be.

26

VOICE FROM ABOVE

Early Friday Morning

Hotel Montana, Port-au-Prince

"Dan. Dan! Can you hear me?"

"Yes?" I was confused. The voice was familiar, but I couldn't place it.

"Dan, I'm coming to get you."

It was Sam, the rescuer who said he would come through the elevator shaft to get me! So much had happened since he'd left to get his equipment that I hadn't really thought about him returning. I tried to guess how long it had been since I had first heard his voice. I couldn't tell. It might have been an hour; it might have been several hours. I had no concept of time.

I realized I was lying on my back, half in and half out of the elevator. *How had I gotten into the lobby?* I wasn't in a safe place. I scrambled back into the elevator. Then I remembered what had just happened. *Had I been in hell, or had I just been hallucinating?*

I stayed near the front edge of the car so I could hear Sam's voice above me. "I'm coming through the elevator shaft, and I'll be down there in just a minute."

When I caught my first glimpse of Sam, it was still dark except for the illumination from his headlamp, which sent a shaft of light in whatever direction his head turned. I watched as he lowered himself between the shaft and the car, using a system of ropes and pulleys. Within a minute or two, he was standing in front of me.

"Here, drink this," he said, handing me a bottle of water and then a flashlight. The water and the light provided instant sanity for me. It didn't matter where I'd been or what had happened to me. At that moment, hope was tangible: a bottle of water, a flashlight, and a way out of the elevator. After having been buried for two and a half days under the Hotel Montana, things were about to change. I couldn't tell if the water was warm or just room temperature, but it didn't matter. As it passed my parched tongue, it felt like I was drinking gold — more precious than words could ever describe. I tasted optimism in the water and drank until I drained the bottle. Then I licked the last drops off my lips.

For the first time, I could really see my surroundings. Everything in the tiny elevator was covered in gray — the walls, the floor, even me. The only patches of color were the rust-colored blotches of dried blood on the walls and the floor where my wounds had come into contact with the surfaces. Even those had a layer of dust on them.

"Are you hurt?" Sam asked.

"I've got a cut on my head, but my leg is worse. It has a big gash, and I think it's broken."

Sam knelt next to me and gently cut off the shirt I had tied around my leg, leaving only a small portion that was embedded in the wound. He tried to pull it out of my leg, but when I winced, he stopped and rewrapped it — this time in bandages.

Though I didn't have my glasses, I could see Sam was also covered in dust. He was dressed in a navy jacket with a fire red Fairfax, Virginia, patch, matching navy pants, and work boots. Dirt smeared his face. The headlamp strapped to his Day-Glo hard hat made me blink every time it flashed in my direction. Like an urban cowboy, he had unhooked and tossed his harness and ropes aside once he was safely on the ground. He was the epitome of every superhero I had ever known. I wondered if his family — and the people of Fairfax — understood what a hero he was. For the first time since the quake,

I felt safe. Someone knew my name, knew where I was, and knew I was alive.

"Were you in the elevator when the quake hit?" Sam asked.

"No, I was out there," I said pointing toward the lobby. I explained how David and I had just entered when the quake hit and how I'd narrowly missed being hit by the wall.

"Did you say there was someone in the other elevator?"

"Yes, my friend Lukeson." I knew Lukeson had to have heard us. "Lukeson, Sam is here to rescue us."

"Dan-yell, I am right here."

As I looked to the far wall, I could see his fingers wiggling, waving at me from a corner of the elevator. Lukeson had seen the light coming from my car and found a spot where he could reach his hand through a small opening between the cars. Sam asked Lukeson if he was injured, then squeezed a bottle of water to him through the opening.

While Lukeson drank, Sam went into the lobby and looked for signs of David but didn't find anything. Then he tried to pop Lukeson's elevator door open by using the "fireman's latch" — a special safety feature used to open elevator doors during an emergency. But it didn't work.

"Look, guys, I need to figure a couple of things out," said Sam. "I have to go back up and consult with my team and grab some more tools. I'll be back in a few minutes. Will you guys be OK?"

After making sure we were both stabilized, Sam laid his finger aside his nose and rose out of the elevator like Santa Claus; or maybe he used the ropes and pulleys. Either way, it was miraculous to see him come and go so easily from the very place that had held me prisoner for so long.

"How are you holding up, Lukeson?"

"I'm better. Thank you, Dan-yell." The water had helped; his voice sounded stronger.

Even though Sam had gone back up the shaft, he and his partner,

Raul, faithfully kept us updated. Raul relayed messages to us when Sam left. And sometimes Sam stayed and asked Raul to retrieve tools. In any case, Lukeson and I were in constant contact with one or both of them as they made trips back and forth to get the necessary equipment. It was very reassuring.

"Hey, Raul, I need a different saw," Sam shouted, after the one he was using wouldn't cut through the thick metal. Raul then yelled up to Mike, and Mike yelled up to Carlos. The saw was then passed down through the same chain of men. They obviously worked well as a team.

I heard Sam yell up the shaft again. "The power isn't on!"

Sometimes there was a wait while another rescuer finished using the power supply with a different tool. The message would go up through the same channels until someone plugged it in or turned it on. Then the saw blades would start moving. But this time, shortly after they started, they stopped.

"What's going on?" Sam yelled.

"You can't use the saw. The French team said they don't want us sawing right now," came the reply.

"Well, tell Evan to tell Mike that I just need fifteen minutes, and I'll have access to a survivor. Tell the French to let me have access. I need to get this guy out. He has serious injuries."

Listening to Sam and his team convinced me that the chaos I had imagined outside on the rubble pile was very real. But when I was trapped in complete darkness, it was hard to tell what was real and what was my imagination. What had happened to me? *Had I really died and gone to hell, or was it some kind of hallucination?*

I believe in the existence of Satan, an evil power who would do anything to keep me from trusting God. I wouldn't put it past him to try to mess with my mind and cause me to despair. But why had I so quickly abandoned the complete trust I had in God during my worship time? Did Satan have that much power to influence me?

Maybe it was a physical thing? Perhaps the lack of food and water had caused me to lose control over my mind. I'd fought so hard for control over my thoughts, but I knew from reading other survival stories that there came a point when intention didn't matter anymore — the body would break down until the person no longer had control over his body or his mind. I hated to think that after trying so hard, I had lost control in the final moments.

My best guess is that it was some combination of both a physical breakdown and a spiritual attack. As my body deteriorated to the point where I couldn't control it, my thoughts were more susceptible to the darkness than they'd ever been. While I would probably never be completely sure of what really happened, I thanked God for bringing me through.

There was more back-and-forth between rescue team members, and then Sam updated me. "The French are worried about the vibrations and the sound the saws make. They're worried about debris falling down the shaft and compromising their work with a survivor in another area." Earlier, Sam had wanted to cut a hole two stories above where the shaft was bent, but the French had prevented him from doing it; instead, he had to work through the entire length of the six-story shaft. I could hear the frustration in his voice. "Those French — they're not letting us do what we need to do."

I wasn't happy with the French either. If they hadn't lost the list, I may have been out of here by now. It's not that I was underestimating what they did or that I wasn't thankful — they had been heroic and saved my friends, and I appreciated that. But if just *one* person on that team had remembered that Lukeson and I were here and had passed on that information, there would be no need for the equipment that caused the vibrations they were now so worried about. But in the midst of unknown dangers and complexities these men were risking their lives for others like me. Pressures of time and safety weighed down every task and decision. I needed to extend them more grace; my knowledge of their challenges was simplistic and limited.

I was glad Sam was in charge of my rescue now; his priorities and commitment to me were clear. I trusted he would do whatever he had to do to get us out.

Earlier, Sam had asked me if he could contact someone to let them know I was here. I had given him Christy's name and phone number, as well as Compassion's info and who to contact there. "Did you get ahold of Christy or someone at my office?" I asked.

"I've passed on the information to our contact at the embassy. Those calls are all routed through them. If they haven't taken care of it yet, they soon will," said Sam.

I relaxed a bit more, knowing that Christy would soon know I was alive.

"We're going to have to wait a few minutes until we work things out with the French team. Is there anything I can get you while we wait?" Sam asked.

"Can I have a granola bar? That's what I'd really like — just something to eat."

"Yeah, totally. I'll get that for you." Sam climbed partway up the elevator to bring down some supplies. I could hear him calling up to his buddies, and a few minutes later, he dropped back down into my elevator. "I'm sorry. The medic who is waiting for you said you couldn't have any food." I knew what that meant. They were taking me into surgery as soon as I got out. I was disappointed, but I understood.

Sam asked me to step outside of the elevator so he could cut a hole in the ceiling. But the saw made so much noise, and such a mess, he decided it would be faster and easier to take Lukeson and me out through the sidewalls of our elevator cars rather than the top. The sides were made of a thinner metal that was much easier to saw through.

"Have you guys seen each other yet?" Sam asked.

I hobbled over to Lukeson's side of the car and shined my flashlight on the hole where Lukeson had stuck his fingers through earlier. Lukeson stuck his head as high as he could, so he could see out his hole, and I did the same thing. Though I could barely see his face, I could tell his dark eyes were bright, reflecting the happiness in his voice. He could barely see my face, but the connection still felt good for both of us.

"The hole where I entered the shaft isn't as big as we need it to to get you guys out," Sam said. "Instead, we're going to have to take you the whole length of the shaft. It's not straight up and down; it bent into an L-shape about two stories above you. This means I'm going to need you to help guide yourselves through a maze of obstacles and debris. Do you think you can both do that?"

"Yes!" I said.

"I can do dat!"

"We're going to get you out of here first, Lukeson," Sam said.

I was happy to hear Lukeson was getting out first because he was in worse shape than I was. I lay down on the floor and waited for my turn. I still felt really weak.

Sam squeezed back into the shaft between our elevators and cut a big hole in the side of Lukeson's. Once Sam had access to Lukeson, he climbed in, helped Lukeson get strapped into a harness, then guided him out through the hole in the elevator. Using the pulleys, the team then hoisted Lukeson up and out through the shaft. It took them about twenty minutes to get Lukeson out.

Then Sam came back down the shaft and cut a hole large enough for me to fit through in the side of my elevator.

Sam looked me in the eye and said, "We could take another five hours or so to cut a bigger hole we could pull you through, or if you're willing to guide yourself through the shaft, we can take you now."

"Take me now! I can do it. I have some strength left in my arms, even if my legs are weak."

"OK. Let's do it!"

He helped me into an L-shaped seat. It was made of thick, padded canvas with some kind of hard metal or plastic on the inside. It had a stiff neck brace and huge straps that Sam used to secure me in place.

"I'm going to be down here for a little while," Sam said. "Is there anything else I can do for you while I'm here?"

"Please look for David — any signs of David." I didn't have much hope that he would still be found alive, but I wanted to do what I could to at least make sure they recovered his body. Based on our earlier conversation, Sam knew how important this was to me. "And second, it's not a big deal, but could you look for my backpack?"

Sam promised me he would do both. Then with a tug on the chain, and Sam guiding me through the hole, I started to move up and out of the elevator.

In my simplistic view, I imagined the shaft was like those I'd seen in the movies — a vertical tunnel with a ladder running up each of the side walls. When Sam asked me if I could guide myself through it, I didn't think it would be a problem. I imagined using my arms to help pull myself up, rung by rung, through the length of the shaft.

But the experience was very different, and considerably more dangerous. The shaft was a tight squeeze. It went straight up for several stories, then abruptly took a sharp left turn at the bend. Broken concrete and thick metal spikes protruding from the walls made the opening in the center of the passage so narrow that there was barely room for one person at a time to slip through.

I had pictured just Sam and Raul being involved in my rescue, but I could see there were many rescuers involved. As I passed by each one, they smiled and said encouraging things. Just a few hours ago, I had questioned the rescuers' competence, their caring spirit, and their commitment to rescue survivors like Lukeson and me. We thought we had been abandoned, but now here were eight or ten guys risking their lives to get me out. They seemed so happy to see me. I was deeply moved and thanked each one for their help.

Because of the tight passage, the rescuers stood in corners or hung off crevices, like Spiderman, to give me enough room to pass. There was a pulley at the top, but they were also manually pulling me from man to man. As I passed by each one, they smiled and encouraged me. They grabbed my arms as they hoisted and guided me through each obstacle, and I used my hands to maneuver around the debris. Throughout the process, they called out useful advice to help me navigate the dangers.

"You're going to have to twist your body about forty-five degrees to make it through this next part."

"Careful, there are metal rods sticking out on your left. Don't let 'em slice you."

It was dangerous and slow going. I'd bump against one wall, then bump the debris on the other side. I grabbed the hands of rescuers and pulled myself up past the next obstacle. Every few feet, another fireman or rescue worker grabbed my chair to help guide me. They always tried to position me so the cushioned back of the chair shielded me from the worst danger, ensuring the padding would protect me from being hurt.

When I got to where the shaft bent, I had to move out of the chair into a sled so I could make the turn and fit through the final horizontal part of the shaft.

Moving from the chair to the sled seemed dangerous. I had to hang on to the pulley while they got the sled in position. I felt like I might fall right back down to where I'd come from. But these men were professionals. They knew what they were doing, and I trusted them.

The orange sled was made of thick plastic, and it looked like a toboggan. Once in it, they tightened the straps so I was held in place like a mummy. This would help them navigate me through the narrowest parts of the shaft.

Though I couldn't see where I was going as well as I could while in the chair, I could feel the sled begin to move. *Only a few more minutes, and I will be completely out!*

Suddenly, the sled hit something and I could feel myself tipping to the right as it slipped. I heard one of the rescuers yelling. "Hey, you're losing him. You're losing him!"

27

CHRISTY, PART 1: MISSING

Friday, January 15, 5:20 a.m. (MST)

Colorado Springs, Colorado

I roll over and open my blurry eyes. I feel dazed and confused from the sleeping pill I took the night before. I see my mom standing over me in the dark.

"Christy, wake up! The State Department is on the phone!"

I immediately sit up and grab the phone. I had been waiting for this call since the earthquake. My stomach clenched, and my throat tightened — I was afraid of what they were going to say. Were they calling to tell me that Dan's body had been found, crushed in his bed at the Hotel Montana? While that would be unbearable to hear, I had been living on the edge for three days, and I wanted to know the truth — whatever it was.

Tuesday, January 12, 2:30 p.m. (MST)

Nathan was asleep at last. I took an extra minute to peek at his small, exhausted body and smiled at his angelic face framed by sweaty little curls. I had put him down for his nap and sang to him until sleep overtook him. I closed his door and headed downstairs to find Josh so we could start his homeschool lessons. That's when my phone rang. It was Dan. He'd left on Sunday for Miami and then on to Haiti. Today he was working in the slums with mothers and their babies. I couldn't wait to hear what he had to say.

"Hello?"

"Hi, honey! How was your day? Did you get the check picked up and deposited?"

"Yeah, I did it this morning."

"Thanks. How's your day going?"

"Josh and Nathan did the funniest thing this morning. I won't go into all the details; I'll save that for when you get back. How do you like Haiti?"

Dan briefly told me how Haiti looked like a tropical paradise, but it was burdened with extreme poverty. It reminded me of why he was there and of the important work he was doing on behalf of Compassion.

"David and I are headed back to the hotel. We're pretty tired, so we'll probably lie down for a few minutes and get dinner after that. I'll call you later tonight when I can talk more."

"OK. I'm taking the boys to gym class and then to swimming, so it will be late by the time we're back. Talk to you then."

"Love you."

"Love you too."

Josh and I worked on schoolwork until Nathan woke from his nap. I let them play for a few minutes while I packed Josh's gym bag, grabbed a few toys for Nathan, and gathered the boys' swimming gear. Then I wrangled both boys toward the car.

———

The gym class served two purposes. First, it counted as a PE credit for Josh's homeschooling education. Second, it was a social hour for me. We'd been attending the same class, with the same moms and kids, for several years and had all been friends for a long time. While our older kids participated in the class, we did our best to keep our younger kids entertained as we caught up on each other's lives. It was one of my favorite times of the week.

As the class finished up, my phone rang again. It was my sister.

"Get your socks and shoes on while I talk to Aunt Valerie," I told Nathan. "Hey, Valerie," I said as I answered the phone.

"Christy, have you heard from Dan?"

"Yes, I just talked to him a little bit ago. Why?"

"Is he OK?"

"I think so. What's the matter?"

"Well," she said hesitantly, "I just saw on the news that there's been a horrible earthquake in Port-au-Prince, Haiti. Have you heard from Dan?" she asked again.

"I wasn't expecting to. He's going to call me tonight."

"OK, listen, Christy. Why don't you try to call him now and then call me back and let me know."

I hung up and dialed Dan.

"This number is no longer in service," played the recorded message.

That's odd. I tried again.

Same message.

Maybe the earthquake had taken out the cell phone towers. That would explain why my calls weren't getting through to Dan, or his to me.

I was texting Dan when my friend Holly walked over. She could tell something was wrong. "Dan is in Haiti, and there has been an earthquake. I can't get ahold of him."

"Oh, Christy!" I could see a worry in her eyes that I wasn't yet feeling. "Let's stop and pray."

As Holly gathered our friends and prayed for Dan, I tried to let the news sink in. I had very little to go on. I knew Dan; if there was an earthquake, he would help rescue survivors. He'd call me when he could.

Holly finished her prayer. "Amen."

"Thanks," I mumbled, my thoughts elsewhere as I gathered the boys and escorted them to the car.

There was no point in changing our schedule. Our home phone was my cell phone. If Dan tried to call, he could reach me wherever I was. I decided to take the boys to the swimming class. Holly followed behind us in her car. She'd wanted to check out the class for her boys and thought I might need a friend.

On the drive over, I called my parents and told them what I knew and asked if they could watch the news to see what they could learn. I didn't want the radio on because I didn't want the boys to hear anything until I had more information.

During the drive, Rick, one of Dan's superiors from Compassion, called.

"Have you heard from Dan?" he asked.

"No, but I've heard about the earthquake."

"All communications are down, so we haven't heard anything either. Do you have his itinerary?"

"No. I just have his flight schedule."

"Do you know where he is staying?"

"No."

"Do you know if he has a satellite phone with him?"

"No, he doesn't."

"Do you know what he was doing today?"

"He was working in the slums earlier today. When I talked to him a couple of hours ago, he was headed back to the hotel."

"Would you give us permission to break into his work computer to see if we can find anything to help us identify where he is?"

"Yes!"

Rick promised to call me if he got any new information and left me his number so I could do the same.

By the time we arrived at swimming, I was feeling pretty helpless. *What could I do?* Holly pulled me aside while the boys were swimming.

"Christy, I talked to my husband, and he saw reports about the earthquake on the news. It was a 7.0 quake centered in Port-au-Prince. Early word is that the hospital and a hotel — the Hotel Montana — have collapsed. Was that Dan's hotel?" asked Holly.

"I don't think so. He mentioned a hotel, but I think it had a French-sounding name."

As she continued to give me the update, I could see in her eyes how concerned she was. *Did I look that concerned? Should I be more upset?* I was feeling numb; removed from the situation. This kind of thing doesn't happen to people I knew, let alone to me. Words like *collapsed* and *thousands suspected dead* echoed in my ears. I continued to call and text Dan.

Still no reply.

On the way home from swimming, I called Dan's mom. The boys were laughing and talking in the backseat, so I kept my voice low as I filled her in on what I knew. She had heard about the earthquake but hadn't realized Dan was in Port-au-Prince.

"I haven't heard from him, and I don't know if he is dead or alive," I said growing more anxious as I talked.

"Oh, Christy ..."

Hearing the sadness in her voice pricked a hole in my emotional dam. I couldn't hold back the tears anymore, and I started to cry.

The boys had stopped playing and overheard some of what we were talking about. I let Dan's mom go, promising to call her back when I had more news.

As soon as I placed my phone in the cup holder, Josh, our six-year-old, said, "Where's Daddy?"

I took a deep breath. "I'm not sure. No one can find him. But Jesus is taking care of him." The answer seemed to satisfy him. I needed to be more careful around the boys.

As we pulled into the driveway, Nathan, who was three, saw Dan's car and said, "Oh no, Mommy! Daddy beat us home. See, there's his car!"

"No, he's not home, Nathan," Josh said harshly. "Daddy's dead. We don't have a daddy anymore."

"Nooo! I want my daddy!" Nathan started to wail. "I love my daddy! I need my daddy!"

Father, help me know what to do; what to say to the boys.

Josh looks a lot like Dan, but he has my emotional insides. He is passionate, and everything is either great or awful. There was very little in-between for him. Usually, I tried to prepare him to hear difficult things by breaking it to him gently so we could talk about it together.

I put the car in park, turned off the engine, and turned to look at the boys.

Nathan stared at me, his big blue eyes dripping with tears. He was so young and had such a tender little heart. *How could he understand this?*

What do I say without scaring them? I couldn't tell them Daddy might be hurt, or worse, Daddy might be dead. I needed to protect them, but I also couldn't lie and say everything was all right, because it wasn't.

"Boys, Daddy is with Jesus. He might be in heaven; or he might be in Haiti, but he is in Jesus' hands. Let's pray for Daddy."

The three of us bowed our heads, and I led the boys in prayer:

Dear Jesus, please help Daddy. Please help people find him, and help him be able to call us so we know he's OK. If he is helping others, please help him be safe. Thank you that you are with him where he is, in heaven or Haiti. Amen.

I could hear their sweet voices echo mine. "Amen."

I opened the doors and helped them get out of their seats. "OK, boys, I need you to help me. Josh, you go get your pajamas on, and Nathan, can you pick out some books to read? I have to make a few phone calls."

———

At eight fifty, I wrote the following update on my Facebook page, a page I hadn't used in months:

Dear Friends, Dan is in Port-au-Prince, Haiti, where they've had today the largest recorded earthquake ever in Haiti. No one is able to find Dan. No one is able to reach him, as there are huge blackouts. No one is able to get downtown to where his hotel was. Please pray for his life. Please pray that his life was spared. Thank you.

Around nine thirty, my parents came over. The boys were supposed to be in bed with lights out at eight. I had been so busy answering the phone that I had let them run wild. My parents offered to get the boys ready for bed, and I was grateful for the help. When I went to tuck them in, I did what we always did when Dan was gone. "When is Daddy coming home?" I asked the boys.

"Friday!" said Josh.

"That's right. How many days until Friday?"

We counted on our fingers how many more days until Daddy would be home. Three days. I prayed that our count would be right.

———

The rest of the night was a blur. So many people called I lost track of who I'd talked to and who I hadn't. People called with hopeful and depressing news, good information and rumors. My head was spinning as I tried to take it all in.

During a break between calls, I Googled hotels that matched the rate Dan told me he'd be paying for his hotel in Port-au-Prince. There was only one hotel that matched — the Hotel Montana. It was the very same hotel that was in the news for how quickly the structure had collapsed. I thought of Dan, returning from his day out and falling asleep in his bed, and then being startled awake long enough to experience the ceiling collapsing on top of him.

Rick told me to call him if I had any news, so even though it was late, I did.

"Dan was staying at the Hotel Montana."

"Are you sure?" asked Rick.

"Yes, and he is probably still there. I talked to him twenty minutes before the quake, and he was on his way back to the hotel. He said he was going to lie down before dinner. Please have someone check the hotel. Maybe he is still in his room."

"We can't reach anyone. We haven't made contact with any of our staff," Rick said. "We're looking at a lot of options, including trying to charter a plane. We have a team in the Dominican Republic, and they're going to try to get across the border."

"Have them check the Hotel Montana for Dan and David," I said before hanging up.

Around 10:30 p.m., I updated my Facebook status again:

> Thanks, friends, for your wonderful messages. I can't tell you how you have helped my heart! Update: so far no American citizen fatalities have been reported, but no one has found Dan yet.

It was late, and the calls had slowed down. When the phone rang with an area code I didn't recognize, I immediately answered.

"Hello. Hello?" All I could hear was static. My heart stopped, and every hair on my body stood up as I strained to hear anything I could through the static. But the line disconnected.

Then the phone rang again from the same number. "Hello." Same thing. All static, no voice. I started yelling into the phone, "Dan! Dan, is this you? Dan, is this you?" My parents came in from the other room and watched helplessly as I continued to yell into the phone. Again the call disconnected.

For a third time, a call came through from the same number. It had to be Dan. Who else would try so hard to get through? This time, I didn't even say hello. "Dan, I can't hear you. Please just scream yes over and over again, and hopefully I will hear you and know you're OK."

But once again the call disconnected. I was surprised at how much I needed the caller to be Dan.

Finally, the phone rang a fourth time, but as soon as I heard the voice on the other end, I knew it wasn't Dan. It was Dustin, Dan's direct supervisor from Compassion.

"Christy, I'm calling from a friend's phone. I'm in California, but

I'm on my way back to Denver. Here's the number where you can reach me if you need me."

I grabbed a pencil, and as I wrote it down, the lead snapped. I had to grab another. Obviously, I was tenser than I realized. I barely paid any attention to what Dustin said. I couldn't. My heart was breaking.

People talk about a broken heart as a metaphorical description, but I felt *real* pain in my chest. Something bad must have happened to Dan, because he would have called me by now. Sure, he would help rescue people, but during the first break he had, he would have called to let me know he was OK. But I hadn't heard a word from him, and that wasn't like Dan. He knew I'd worry, and he'd do whatever he could to get in touch with me.

This was bad.

It was very bad.

I started thinking about what life would be like without Dan. *Could I raise the boys on my own?* Whether I could or couldn't, I didn't want to! I didn't want to do life without him.

God, please help me!

It was nearly midnight. I sent my parents home so I could be alone to cry and pray.

———

Before getting into bed, I pulled Dan's dirty clothes out of the hamper and buried my nose in them, inhaling deeply. I wanted his smell near me. But it wasn't enough. It wasn't him. I wrapped myself in his clothes and tried to feel his arms around me. The fear, worry, and loneliness bubbled to the surface, and I let my tears pour out. I wept like I'd never wept before.

And I prayed. But the more I prayed the less my words made sense. At one point, all I could do was lie prostrate on our bed, crying out, "God, save Dan! Please, God, save Dan!"

During the darkest part of the night, I couldn't picture Dan's face. I prayed, *Please, God, help me remember what Dan looks like.* Immediately, images of his broken body flashed through my mind.

Dan sprawled out with concrete blocks crushing his body, his head. He was lying there dead.

As each image came up, I prayed, *God, please take this picture away.*

And he did. But as one disappeared, a new one replaced it.

Morning couldn't come soon enough.

28

CHRISTY, PART 2:
BOOTS AND GLOVES

Wednesday, January 13

I slept less than twenty minutes all night. Eventually, I traded the charade of sleep for surfing the Internet. By 5:30 a.m., I had scoured most of the news sites, but there was still very little information coming in from Haiti. I called Rick from Compassion. "Have you heard anything yet?"

"No, but let me call you when I get into the office. Maybe I'll know more then."

Overnight, we'd put Dan on the State Department's missing persons list. It had taken two tries, but at least I knew he was on the list, and now they'd look for him.

My parents came over early and took the boys to their house for breakfast. I'd planned to resume our normal schedule but quickly realized that if I was out and got a call with bad news, I'd completely crumble. There would be no way I could drive home. It was safer to stay put.

———

Throughout the day, I found it hard to focus. My mind flitted from taking care of the boys to thoughts of what I'd do if Dan never returned. I could feel my heart racing and I knew I needed to eat, but even the thought of food made my already churning stomach churn even more.

I continued to get calls from family and friends asking for updates. My sister Valerie made connections for me as we searched everywhere we could for information. A State Department representative called to say that a plane was leaving the Dominican Republic with 130 American evacuees headed back to the States. He was going to try to get a copy of the passenger list. He promised to call if he saw Dan's name on it.

He never called back.

While the boys were at my parents' house, I briefly turned on the TV. There were breaking news specials on the earthquake in Haiti. They showed bodies lining both sides of the streets. The newscaster said there were so many bodies that they were running out of sheets to cover them. I looked at the grotesque expressions on the lifeless faces — vacant eyes open and staring, twisted mouths with flies buzzing around, broken bones protruding from stiffening limbs.

I turned off the TV.

Later that afternoon, the phone rang from an unknown number. The area code was 202 — Washington, D.C. I swallowed hard as I picked up the phone.

"Hello?"

"I need to speak to the next of kin for Daniel Woolley."

"This is his wife." I held my breath.

"This is the U.S. State Department calling, and we need some information from you."

"Yes?"

"Mrs. Woolley, can you give us a description of Dan and what he might be wearing?"

I exhaled slowly. I was glad I had helped Dan pack his suitcase on

Sunday before he left because I knew exactly what he had with him. "He will probably be wearing a black T-shirt with a button-down shirt over the top. Most likely he'll have on jeans or khaki pants. He wears yellow and black tennis shoes. He wears glasses, but he probably won't have them on because he takes them off when he sleeps. He has a ring on each hand — um, what else? That's all I can think of."

"OK, Mrs. Woolley. One more question."

"Sure, what is it?" It felt good to actively contribute to finding him, even if it was over the phone, from thousands of miles away.

"Does Dan have any identifying scars or marks on his limbs?"

I was stunned.

My mind flashed back to the bodies I had seen earlier on TV. I knew what they were asking. They wanted to be able to identify his *body parts* in case they only found pieces of him.

Bile rose in my throat, and I fought the urge to throw up.

Earlier in the day, Dan's sister mentioned that she had a few media connections. We discussed whether it made sense to contact them. Ultimately, we thought it might help to get Dan's face and story out to the public. If nothing else, it would make the journalists working in Haiti aware of him. Perhaps one of them would recognize Dan.

Good Morning America was the first to call. They asked if they could come to the house and interview me later in the evening. I agreed. I was willing to do whatever it took to help Dan get home, and I knew that few things attract more attention than a desperate wife.

I got the kids bathed, and my dad helped me clean the house before the crew arrived. It was a helpful distraction — it felt good to have something tangible to focus on.

The interview went well, and they planned to air it the next morning. I felt like I'd honored Dan, and I'd honored God with the things I said. By putting Dan's picture on TV, I hoped someone would recognize him, or at least turn up the heat in the search for his body.

Before the producer left, she asked if I would send her some pictures of Dan so they could put them up on television. Looking for pictures was a harder task than I thought — Dan was usually the photographer so he wasn't in most of our photos. I spent several hours trying to find current pictures of Dan and our family. Once I found a few, I sent them to the media contacts I had. I hoped it would keep Dan in their minds as they looked for survivors.

The TV was on until one in the morning, and then I turned out the lights and fell into a restless sleep. But an hour later, I woke up feeling like I was being smothered. I couldn't breathe, and my heart was racing. I was drenched in sweat and felt like I was losing control. It was a full-blown panic attack.

My thoughts became obsessed with our finances, which I knew very little about. I'd asked Dan to put all of the financial information in one place so I'd have access to it if I needed it, but he had neglected to do it before he left. Things had to be particularly tenuous right now because Dan had called on Tuesday to make sure I deposited a check. Dan got paid on Friday, but I had no idea what bills were due. I didn't know where to go or how to find out. *What if we lost the house because I didn't know where to send the house payment?* I knew where we banked and where Dan kept the checkbook, but that was all. My throat tightened, and it was harder to take deep breaths.

Maybe we could get through life without Dan, but how? I would move in with my parents, and they could help me raise the boys. But I would have to get a job, which meant I'd have to give up homeschooling. That would add to my heartaches.

I stayed up the rest of the night trying to plan for a future without Dan.

Thursday, January 14

I had been praying intermittently all night, but as morning neared I wondered, *How should I pray?* God, in his sovereignty, had already decided Dan's fate. *Would my prayers change his mind?* I knew that he asks us to lay all of our burdens before him and that he always listens to our prayers. So I decided to pray what I desired, which was Dan's safe return to me. I trusted that, in his love for us, God would make the best decision for our family, even if that meant calling Dan to heaven. But it was hard to imagine that this outcome would be the best for us.

Early in the morning, my mom burst into my room crying. A representative of the State Department had called and said I needed to send a very specifically worded e-mail to the State Department so they could forward it to the embassy in the Dominican Republic. There was no explanation of why this was needed. I was afraid it was because they had found his body and wanted to make sure they had the correct next-of-kin information.

I had been awake all night anyway, so I scrambled out of bed and headed to the computer and typed: *I am Christina Schroeder Woolley, and I am the next of kin of Daniel William Woolley.* I listed his Social Security number, passport number, a description, and my contact information. And then I clicked Send.

We were told they would call within two hours.

Had they found Dan's body? Or was he on a plane bound for Miami? I sat on the couch with my knees under my chin and wouldn't let anyone touch me. I didn't watch *Good Morning America* — I was too upset, and I didn't need to see myself on TV. I just rocked back and forth and cried, cradling the phone, waiting for the official word.

I thought about the day ahead. *How can I make it through today?* I wanted to be a strong mommy for Josh and Nate, but I was falling apart. I desperately needed God's strength. I knew I couldn't make it through this day without him.

I updated my Facebook status:

I was interviewed by *Good Morning America*. They put up several pictures of Dan, and some of the media on the ground have a picture of him. People are looking for him. No news from Dan yet. Haiti is starting to fly Americans out to Cuba, the DR, and Miami. They have not released names of survivors yet.

And a minute later I updated it again:

As lists of survivors are posted all over the place, please wait for the State Department's list. That will be the most accurate. There are so many rumors. My heart has stopped and started several times this morning as we read lists of the found and as I wait for a call from the State Dept. Please pray for me as I need to be a mommy for worried boys today and am having trouble keeping myself together.

The boys slept in, since they had been up late the night before. When they woke up, Mom took the kids to her house, and Dad stayed with me.

The two-hour mark had barely passed when my phone rang.

It was Valerie. "Christy, I think I saw him. I think I saw him on *Good Morning America*."

"What?"

"They showed people at the airport, and I think I saw Dan at the airport waiting for a flight out."

I paced the floor, waiting for the phone call saying they had found his body, while simultaneously hoping he was at the airport catching a flight home. Then I couldn't wait any longer; it had been three hours and no phone call! I had to do something. A friend had taped the *Good Morning America* segment for me, so I grabbed a magnifying glass out of our homeschooling supplies and asked Mom to drive me to my friend's house. Dad stayed with the boys.

———

I watched the Haiti segment in slow motion on my friend's big-screen TV. I saw him too — even without the magnifying glass! A man who looked like Dan lifted a TV camera and put it on his shoulder.

Maybe Dan's alive! I didn't realize how erratically I was behaving until I saw the look on my mom's face.

I hadn't gotten dressed. I was still in a combination of Dan's dirty clothes and the same T-shirt I had worn since Tuesday. My hair was in a hat, and I was so emotional I was shaking. Mom drove me back home.

The possibility of Dan being at the airport gave me the hope I needed to face the day. I updated my Facebook status again:

> I talked with ABC news in NY, and they are going to try to pan slowly across the Americans who are at the Haiti airport. If anyone is watching ABC, would you please look for Dan and let me know if you see him? Thanks!

And then a minute later:

> He may have a huge movie camera on his shoulder or a camera with a telephoto lens. Thanks so much!

Because of the media coverage, more people had learned about Dan. We were receiving messages from friends and churches all over the world who were praying for Dan. The possible glimpse of Dan on TV, as well as the fact that the State Department hadn't called back, left me with more hope than I'd had since the earthquake. But the reality that we still hadn't heard anything except speculation left me exhausted.

"Christy, you have to eat something," my mom coaxed.

I agreed. I hadn't eaten a full meal since noon on Tuesday, over forty-eight hours ago.

I joined my family at my parents' house next door for a late dinner. It was the first time since the earthquake that we had all sat down together to talk. As I told them about how worried I was and my fears for the future, they tried to encourage me. "Christy, you are not alone in this. You don't ever have to handle anything alone. We will help you no matter what happens."

We were still sitting at the table when my phone rang at around seven thirty. It was Rick from Compassion. "Christy, have you heard anything?" It was the standard greeting we both used.

"No." I stood up from the table and walked back to our house while I talked. "Have you found any of the Compassion staff in Haiti?"

"Well, that's why I was calling. We've located Dan's driver, Ephraim, and he's alive. He said he dropped Dan and David off at the front of the Hotel Montana minutes before the quake. So we know for sure they were at the hotel."

I don't remember ending the conversation or hanging up the phone, but I must have. Dan couldn't be at the airport. He had walked into the Hotel Montana just in time for it to collapse on top of him.

I crumbled in the middle of my kitchen floor and cried out to God in anger. I needed to be honest about my rage, worry, and hope-lessness. And I needed to express it, even if it was directed at God. So I let him have it.

You did this to him. You lined everything up perfectly for Dan's death. First, the timing of his trip was changed. He wasn't even sup-posed to be in Haiti this week! Then, at the last minute, his hotel reservation was switched to the Hotel Montana. And then you made sure he walked into the lobby seconds before it collapsed. Thanks. Thanks a lot for doing this to us.

I was sarcastic, and I'm never sarcastic. But I was so angry and frightened that I didn't hold back. Some might have looked at me and thought I was crazy for yelling at God, but I had never been more sane. One of the most valuable lessons I'd learned through my depression was that God stayed with me and that he loved me, no matter what. There was no point in trying to hide my anger and frustration from him. He already knew about it. If I said it out loud, at least our relationship was honest and authentic. I'd spent too many years hiding my real feelings. Though it wasn't pretty, it was real. And God was real. I could yell at him because God already knew my thoughts. There was no point in lying about how I felt.

Thanks for working this out so I don't have a husband. How am I supposed to make it now? You gave me a husband, and we became one. How can you now ask me to rip myself in half?

During my rage, I felt like I had to remind my heart to beat and my lungs to breathe. I hadn't had anything to drink all day, and I had only nibbled on my dinner.

By the time my dad found me, I was a mess.

"If Dan doesn't make it out, you and Mom are going to have to adopt our kids and raise them," I said.

Dad tried to comfort me, but I wouldn't let him.

"I just need to know whether he is dead or alive. I need to know something tomorrow. I can't keep going on like this."

Mom came over with the kids, and I stayed in the bedroom until she had them upstairs. I didn't want them to see me this upset. She got them into their pj's and tucked them in. It was the first time ever that they'd gone to bed without me being the one to kiss them good night.

Mom expressed concern about how little sleep I had been getting, and she suggested I take a sleeping pill.

"No. I need to be alert for whatever happens tomorrow."

"Christy, you've barely slept for days. If you want to be ready for whatever happens tomorrow, you need some sleep."

"What if someone calls in the middle of the night? I need to be alert if they call."

"I'll spend the night with you, and I'll get the phone."

I reluctantly agreed.

Friday, January 15, 5:20 a.m. (MST)

As the past sixty or so hours flashed through my mind, I realized it had only been two and a half days since the earthquake, but they had been the longest and most stressful days of my life. As I took the phone from my mom, I knew this call was the one that would change my life forever. My hand shook as I lifted the phone to my ear. "Hello."

"Is this Christina Woolley?"

"Yes."

A nameless female voice from the State Department asked if I was Dan Woolley's next of kin.

"Yes."

"We're calling to tell you that Dan's been found alive."

I sucked in my breath and then let it all out in one loud cry. "He's alive?"

"He was alive at the time we got this information. That was approximately ten hours ago. Rescuers found a Dan Woolley buried in an elevator shaft inside the rubble of what used to be the Hotel Montana."

"So he's still there? In the elevator?"

"We don't have any more information, ma'am."

"Did he respond? When they asked his name, could he speak? Is anyone working to get him out?" My questions came faster than her answers.

"I don't know. This is all the information I have at this time."

I thanked her and hung up the phone. I sat in bed, stunned. Mom hugged me and then went to call the rest of the family. *Now what?*

Then I knew.

I went to the closet and pulled out my suitcase and started throwing things in — finishing with my hiking boots and work gloves. Then I grabbed a change of clothes for Dan.

My parents and sister, Anna, rushed in.

"He's alive!" I said as I hugged them. Then I pulled away and went back to packing my suitcase. "He's buried in an elevator, and they're not sure when or if they can get him out."

"So what are you doing?"

"I'm going to Haiti."

Incredulous, they asked, "What will you do when you get there?"

"I'm going to stand next to the rubble until they get him out. If I have to, I'll dig him out with my bare hands."

29

REUNITED

Dan

My helmet had a headlamp, so it wasn't completely dark in the elevator shaft. I turned my head slightly in each direction until I could see the problem. There were metal bars that ran parallel along the elevator shaft. Rescuers had been pushing the sled I was strapped to along these rods to help manage my weight and keep me from slipping into a more treacherous part of the shaft. One of the edges of the sled slipped off the makeshift track, and they started to lose their grip on me.

A rescuer yelled again, "You're losing him. Get him back above those bars!"

Additional hands reached down from rescuers perched above me, and with lots of grunting and a few expletives, they lifted the tilting sled and stabilized it back onto the track. My journey through the shaft continued.

After I'd moved a few more body lengths, someone said, "Dan, if you look back over your left shoulder, you'll see sunlight." I tilted my head back. Immediately, I could feel the heat of the sun on my face. I blinked from the brightness, but I didn't look away. I couldn't — I wouldn't — take my eyes off that blessed, beautiful sun. I stared until green spots danced in front of my eyes.

Thank you, Jesus! I prayed through my tears. *I never thought I would see the sun again. But you watched over me, protected me, and now you rescued me!*

The sun brought out a visceral, energetic feeling in me. What a glorious reminder that I was out of the dark abyss! I would soon be back with my family, with new opportunities to love them. God had a plan for me, and I was determined to spend the rest of my life fulfilling it.

Christy

January 15, Friday Morning

I didn't really think I could move six stories of hotel rubble by myself, but I was savvy enough to know that a desperate wife trying to dig her husband out of the debris would attract a lot of media attention. That could generate help to get Dan rescued.

The next few hours flew by. A friend from church helped me finish packing, and I updated my status on Facebook, asking whether anyone was willing to purchase a ticket for me to Haiti. Three offers from friends came through in a matter of minutes, but when Compassion called, they took care of it.

Saying good-bye to the boys was hard. Nathan had been following me around the house while I packed. He figured out I was leaving.

"Where you goin', Mommy?"

I bent down and kissed him. "I am going to get Daddy and bring him home. You get to stay with Nana and Grandpa!"

I looked for Josh but couldn't find him.

"He's fine," Mom said. "He's upstairs in his room playing with Legos."

When I went to his room to say good-bye, he was hiding. When I found him, he was crying.

"What's wrong, Josh? Why were you hiding?" I asked.

"Daddy isn't coming home. All of his bones are broken."

I knew that I'd never fully explained to Josh that Dan had been in an earthquake and what that meant — I'd only told him we couldn't find Daddy.

"Oh, Josh!" I grabbed him and hugged him to my chest. I told him that I had gotten a call that his dad was still alive. "Honey, we don't know if Daddy is hurt. That's why I am going to get him. I'll be gone for a couple of days. I'm not sure when I'm coming back, but I *am* coming back, and I'll bring Daddy home."

As soon as he was reassured, I dashed out the door, calling to my mom as I left, "Give the kids whatever they want." I thought how Dan would laugh if he knew I said that. I *never* said things like that.

Local reporters stood in the front yard as I left. I didn't have time to talk to them. I said a few hurried words on my way to the car, but I couldn't stop to answer any questions. I probably didn't have the answers anyway.

I had very little money and even fewer plans. I couldn't find my passport, but I had a ticket from Colorado Springs to Dallas to Miami. My plan was to catch a ride to Haiti or maybe the Dominican Republic with a news crew out of Miami. A reporter thought he could pull some strings and get me into Haiti.

I mentally ticked off the hours since the representative from the State Department said they had heard from Dan. It had now been fifteen hours since the rescuers reported Dan was alive. I had no idea how he was now, but I was getting closer to finding out.

Hang on, Dan! I'm coming!

Dan

I knew I had emerged from the building when I could feel the sunlight on every part of my body. It was confirmed when I heard the clicks of dozens of cameras and saw photographers and reporters lined up on both sides of me. I heard people talking excitedly. Some asked me questions, but they weren't all speaking English, and I couldn't understand what they were saying. Within seconds of my exit, a medic started an IV. Someone was cutting through my khakis — and not just cutting through them, but cutting them off completely. I tried to sit up in the sled to see what they were doing. When I looked down, my pants were gone, and all I could see were my boxers. *I guess now isn't the time to worry about modesty.*

Medics swarmed around my leg, examining my wound. They poked and prodded as they tried to see what was under the bandage, and then decided it was best to leave it wrapped.

About this time, I noticed a tall Haitian man walking toward me. His posture was so erect it was almost stiff. He seemed so formal that he had a regal look to him. His kind eyes connected with mine, and I watched his already big smile grow even wider. He bent over me and placed his hand on my face.

"Hello, Dan-yell!"

"Lukeson! So glad to meet you, man!"

It was such a tender moment, but so appropriate for what we'd been through together. I remembered all of the ways we had encouraged each other, the times he'd asked how I was doing, and the songs we sang together. Finally I could see his face, and he could see mine. And his face was beautiful.

I started to worry that my injuries were more severe than I'd thought. It was now obvious they had taken Lukeson out first not because he was more injured but because he was in better health.

The medic asked everyone to step back while they transferred me to a gurney. "Make sure I get your address," I told Lukeson as they loaded me into the back of an old van that a volunteer had converted into a makeshift ambulance. They were preparing to shut the doors when I heard a man yell.

"Wait!"

It was Sam.

He stepped into the van and said, "Hey, look what I found."

"That's my backpack!" It shouldn't have been a big deal, but it was, and I was glad to get it back. I shook Sam's hand and thanked him again. In a flash, he was gone and the medic was by my side. Someone closed the doors, and I felt the engine start.

I obviously had little control over where they were taking me, and

I didn't want to insult anyone, but I was worried about how safe a Haitian hospital would be, given the situation.

"Are you taking me to the hospital?"

"No, we're taking you to the U.S. Embassy. Then you're going to be medevaced out by military transport."

The next thing I remember was lying on a stretcher at the embassy. Volunteer doctors readied me for a flight to Miami.

"My biggest concern right now is that you are at risk for kidney failure because of the dehydration," said the doctor who first looked me over. But after examining me, he added, "I'm also worried about your leg wound and the likelihood of infection. The laceration extends through your muscle and nerves all the way to the bone. You'll need surgery when you get to Miami." He gave some instructions to a nurse, and then he was on to the next bed.

Things moved fast and with military precision. Minutes later, I was flying in a helicopter to the Dominican Republic; then a military transport plane brought me to Miami, followed by an ambulance ride from the plane to a waiting helicopter that delivered me to the hospital. Before I knew it, I was in the Ryder Trauma Center at Miami's Jackson Memorial Hospital. I was admitted to the hospital at 4:53 p.m., exactly three days, to the minute, after the earthquake.

A social worker who was helping to admit me said, "The doctor will see you in a few minutes. Is there anything I can do for you in the meantime?"

"Please, please call my wife, Christy, and let her know I'm OK."

Christy

When I landed in Dallas, I wanted to call the reporter who was going to help me get into Haiti, but I realized my cell phone battery was almost dead. I needed to charge it first. I searched for an outlet, and when I found one, it was in use. *Great.*

"Excuse me, could I please use this outlet to charge my phone?" The man in the business suit looked up from his computer. He didn't seem too friendly, but I just kept talking. "I'm so sorry. I'm on my way to Haiti, and my husband has been missing since the earthquake — "

"Of course!" he said. Even before I could finish my sentence, he pulled his plug out, and I sat on the floor to charge my phone. Once I got it plugged in, for whatever reason, it still didn't work. I buried my head in my hands. *God, what else could go wrong?*

I held the phone in my hands and felt the vibration before I heard the ring. I looked at the number, and it was from an area code I didn't recognize. I had received a lot of those recently.

"Hello?"

"Is this Christina Woolley?"

Oh, no! Phone conversations that started like this were rarely good. "Yes, this is Christina." I held my breath for whatever came next.

"This is Jackson Memorial Hospital in Miami calling. We wanted to let you know we have your husband, Dan Woolley, and we're treating him."

"Dan is in Miami?"

"Yes."

They had gotten Dan out! And I was headed to Miami too!

But my relief was partially deflated by worry about his medical condition. I had heard that injured Americans were being flown to the Dominican Republic and to Cuba. Only the worst cases were being flown back to the States. My stomach dropped as I realized Dan had to be in really bad shape to be in Miami.

"What are his injuries?"

"I'm sorry, Mrs. Woolley. I can't tell you over the phone."

"Please tell him I'm on my way!"

Thank you, God! Thank you for protecting Dan. And for bringing him safely back to the United States. It is amazing how you work. I am just one plane ride away from seeing him, and while I didn't know it, you did — even before I bought the ticket. Thank you for keeping him alive. Thank you that you are still protecting Dan's health.

I was jittery throughout the flight from Dallas to Miami. The plane just couldn't get there fast enough. *What shape would Dan be in? Would he be missing any limbs? Had he suffered any brain damage?* It didn't matter what state he was in. I would take him home and care for him, no matter what.

The man next to me had been sleeping most of the flight, but when we started our final descent, he woke up. By then, I was pretty frazzled. We started talking, and I told him they'd found Dan, but that I didn't know how badly injured he was.

"Is there anything I can do to help? I'm a manager with American Airlines."

He may have been a manager, but he seemed like an angel to me. "Can you walk me to baggage claim? They let me carry my bag on in Colorado Springs, but in Dallas they made me check it. I'm so nervous, I'm not sure I can read the signs to find baggage claim."

"Of course."

Once we deplaned, he walked me to baggage claim, where unfortunately, there was a forty-five-minute wait for luggage due to a malfunction in the baggage delivery system.

I was supposed to meet a reporter and a representative from Compassion. I turned on my phone to call them, but it was completely dead. I located a plug so I could charge it while I waited for my bag.

As soon as I had plugged it in, I noticed that someone had called and left a voice mail. It was Claudia, a Compassion employee who lived near Miami. I called her back. She was with the reporter, waiting in another part of the airport. She told me to stay where I was, and they would find me.

Dan

The doctor had given me strong painkillers while I was still at the embassy in Haiti. As a result, even hours later, I was still feeling the effects. I felt the grogginess overtake me, only to nod off and then awaken to ask again if anyone had called Christy. Finally, the kind social worker said he wasn't supposed to but would let me use his cell phone anyway. I didn't care how many rules I broke; I wanted to call my wife.

Christy

Before I left Dallas, I made a quick call to my mom and Dan's mom to let them know Dan was in Miami. Now I called Mom to let her know I'd arrived safely. We'd only been talking for a minute when my phone beeped.

"Mom, I'll call you back. Someone's calling on the other line." I glanced at the number. It was a Miami area code. "Hello?"

"Christy, I'm a social worker at Jackson Memorial Hospital in Miami."

"I just got here! I'm in Miami. I'm at the airport waiting for my suitcase. Are you near Dan?"

"Yes, I am standing next to his bed. Hold on."

"Christy? Christy?"

"Dan? Dan! Is this you? Is this really you?" I couldn't believe I was hearing his voice. I'd thought I'd never hear it again. It was such a complicated mixture of emotions. I felt giddy, almost giggly from the joy of connecting with him. We both laughed and cried — mostly cried. My joy was overwhelming, but so was my sadness. Dan's voice was so muted, and he sounded so weak that I couldn't help but be worried about him.

"Dan, are you OK?"

"Yes, I'm OK."

"Are you hurt?"

"My leg hurts a little, but I'll be OK. Just get here soon."

"I'm twenty minutes away. I'll be there as soon as I can."

"I have to go. I love you!"

"I love you. I'm twenty minutes away," I said again. "Hang in there!"

The social worker came back on the line and gave me directions on how to find Dan once I got to the hospital. I promised to get there as soon as I could.

When I hung up the phone, I saw that the camera crew had been filming while I talked to Dan. I hadn't even noticed them. They were with Claudia, the Compassion representative, who had connected with them while I was on the phone.

"Dan's in Miami! He's at the hospital. We need to get a cab and get there as quickly as we can."

"I've got a car parked outside. I'll take you," said Claudia.

Claudia pulled her car around while I waited for my suitcase, and then I met her outside. The crew followed behind in their car. When we got to the hospital, they wouldn't let the crew come in with us, so I left them in the parking lot.

I had to see Dan.

30

SOMETHING GOOD

Dan

I was talking to my mom on another borrowed phone when they finally let Christy in to see me. I looked up when I heard the door open. She took my breath away. I had never seen a more beautiful sight in my life.

She saw me and ran toward my bed. "Dan! Oh, Dan." The social worker assigned to escort her had to run to keep up with her.

When she bent over me, I breathed in her sweet smell. If I had been hooked up to a heart monitor, they would have heard it flatline for a moment as my heart stopped.

I couldn't move my left side, so we did a one-armed hug and kissed. Her lips had never tasted so good. She stroked my face, and I reached up to stroke hers. When she kissed me again, I could taste our salty tears mixing on my lips.

"I love you so much," I said, trying to get a grip on my tears. "I never thought I'd see you again."

"I love you too!"

The social worker standing at the end of my bed said to Christy, "I can only let you stay a minute or two, and then you'll have to leave."

But I didn't want it to end. I couldn't stop staring at Christy. "How are the boys?"

"They're fine. I'll tell you more when we have more time."

I wanted to call them right then, but it was almost eleven o'clock local time — nine o'clock in Colorado — and I knew they would already be in bed.

Christy lifted the sheet from my right arm and saw that it was covered in cuts and bruises. She gently pulled back the sheet and looked at my chest and then pulled it back further to reveal my legs.

I watched her face as she examined by broken body. My chest was covered in lacerations. My leg wound was wrapped in fresh bandages, but my left foot was purple and swollen three times its normal size. My whole left side was severely bruised, especially my shoulder where my backpack had been torn off during the earthquake. I knew I was a mess. I didn't want her to see how cut and bruised I was, but Christy didn't flinch as she examined me from head to toe. All I saw was love mixed with concern.

Christy

A helicopter arrived with a new patient, so they made me leave the trauma unit — and Dan's bedside. I returned to the waiting room and told Claudia about Dan's condition.

I started filling out insurance paperwork and waited for the next chance to see Dan. At about one thirty in the morning, a doctor came out to talk with me.

"We're going to do a series of scans to check for internal bleeding and injuries," he said. "That will happen soon." He looked at his watch. "He will have to have surgery tomorrow morning. And I just want you to know, we'll do everything possible to save his leg."

His leg? Dan could still lose his leg?

I wanted to ask more questions, but the doctor was pulled away by another emergency.

Claudia had arranged for us to spend the night at a nearby hotel. I told her to go on without me; I would spend the night here in the hospital. With a promise to return first thing in the morning, she and her family reluctantly left.

The hospital waiting room was bright with fluorescent lights. The uncomfortable chairs were filling with families of other trauma patients. I lay down on the floor and used my bag as a pillow and tried to let my worn-out mind rest.

At 1:45 a.m. my phone rang. I grabbed it and recognized the Miami area code but not the number.

"Hello?"

"Hi, Christy. This is Dan."

"Dan? *My husband?* Why are you calling? Are you OK?"

"They're going to take me into surgery for my leg."

"Yes, they told me. They'll operate on you later this morning."

"No, Christy. They're taking me into surgery now."

"Now?"

"Yes, it's going to be fine. I just wanted to let you know. I can't talk anymore, but I want you to know I'll be fine, and I love you."

The surgery lasted a couple of hours. I stayed in the waiting room and prayed. When the surgical team finished, the doctor came out again.

"Everything went well. We were able to save his leg. We had to remove a lot of debris from around the bone, but, remarkably, there was no infection."

I burst into tears and silently thanked Jesus for another miracle.

"He's in recovery. When he wakes up, they'll bring him to his room. You can wait for him there."

While I would take Dan home any way I could get him, I knew it was a miracle that he would be coming home with both legs! *Thank you, Jesus!*

The hospital arranged for Dan to have a private room, and I went there to wait for him. It was well after 7:00 a.m. when they finally brought him up to the room. Once the nurses got him settled and the orderlies left, it was the first time we were able to be alone.

We both cried. After the horrifying images that had spun through my mind during the past few days, seeing him alive was truly unbelievable. I had to touch him to know I wasn't dreaming. We kissed and hugged. When that wasn't enough, I climbed into the hospital bed with him and put my head on his chest so I could listen to his heartbeat.

"I thought you were dead," I said as I inhaled the smell of him.

"I thought I was too."

Dan was tired and unable to stay awake for very long. But each time he woke up, he'd tell me another part of his story. Over the next day or so, he described where he was when the ceiling fell. If he'd been an inch to one side or the other, he never would have survived.

When I asked about David, he got very quiet. Slowly and softly he told me what he knew. We were both crying by the time he finished. We held hands and prayed for David's family. My heart ached for them.

Dan told me about finding the elevator and how moving there so quickly helped to protect him when, minutes later, the aftershock knocked down more walls. I was amazed as I listened to him describe how God had saved him and given him resources to protect his life so he could live long enough to be rescued.

With each new detail he revealed, I realized what a miracle it was that he was alive. I couldn't help but see God working through it all. In addition to his severe leg wound, Dan's arms, chest, and back were covered in deep cuts and bruises. He had an open wound on the back of his head. Yet the doctor assured us he would return to full health. So many miraculous things had occurred, and I wanted to make sure I didn't take a single one for granted. Less than forty-eight hours ago, I had been furious with God because I thought he was the one responsible for Dan's death. Now I realized that he was the one responsible for Dan's *life*.

I felt the tears sliding down my cheeks. *God, you were the one who did this. While I was blaming you for everything that happened to Dan, you were involved in the smallest details of helping him to survive and come home. Thank you, God! You orchestrated all of this to save Dan!*

Dan

Now that I had access to electricity, I was able to recharge my camera and download pictures to the laptop, which, amazingly, still worked despite being in my backpack during the earthquake. I showed Christy the pictures I had taken. When I saw them blown up to full size on the screen, I had a new appreciation for the destruction that had taken place and the devastation I had lived through. It was truly a miracle from God that I had made it out alive.

A few days in the hospital without the kids was just what Christy and I needed to reconnect. But my time in the hospital showed me that the hotel walls weren't the only ones that had come tumbling down. Things hadn't been great with Christy and me before I left for Haiti. OK — but not great. I realized that for some time I hadn't shown her, through words, time, and actions, how much I loved and cherished her. We hadn't set aside time for dates and "us" time without the kids. And sometimes we allowed conflicting priorities for time and money to come between us.

But there were other, bigger issues too — like when we let a problem between us fester instead of working to resolve it. Those things, and many more like them, had built walls between us, brick by brick, problem by problem. As a result, we weren't as close as we had once been.

I wasn't surprised, and was actually grateful, when Christy brought it up. "When I didn't think you were coming home, I realized how much I'd let those things build up between us. And I don't want our marriage to be like that anymore."

"I don't either, Christy. I love you too much to have walls between us."

"I love you too, but I've also been deeply hurt by you. I want these walls to stay down too, but I'm afraid ..." I could see a familiar fear creep onto her face.

"I had time to rethink a lot of things, Christy, and I spent a lot of time thinking about us. I want to do things differently in our relationship. I don't want to just settle for an OK marriage."

I knew now that every time Christy said she wanted to talk, and I didn't stop to fully listen, I hurt her. Every time I chose my laptop instead of my wife, my actions told her that she wasn't as important as whatever I was working on.

"I promise, every day, no matter how busy I am or how much work I have to do, I will sit down and have a face-to-face, uninterrupted conversation with you for as long as you want me to. And it won't be a superficial conversation. I really want to know how you're doing and what you're thinking about."

"I think there are things I can do better too," Christy said. "I won't bury my hurt feelings when there's a problem between us. I'll tell you about them so we can resolve the issues."

We both promised to be more patient and understanding with each other. I reached up and pulled her down and kissed her. "I've always loved you, and I've never stopped. I am so sorry that you didn't feel cherished by me, and I am going to spend the rest of my life making sure you have no reason to question the depth of my love."

I could see some of the fear in her eyes melt, but I knew these changes would have to play out in our day-to-day lives before her doubts would completely disappear.

Christy looked me as only she could, deeply and penetrating. "Dan, I love you so much."

"I love you too, Sweet."

"I have one more promise I want to make to you." I watched as a smile slid across her face. "I won't get mad when you leave your clothes on the floor."

We both laughed and cried. I knew we were in for big changes. With renewed commitments to our marriage and rekindled passion, I couldn't wait to see what the years ahead would be like.

Christy

As we boarded the airplane that would take us both home, Dan was moving slowly because of the cast on his leg. The flight attendant took his crutches while I settled in my seat. I looked out the window and saw planes rolling down the runway, gathering speed and taking off into the crisp, blue sky. I thought about the amazing journey we'd been on.

People all around the world had been praying for Dan. I would ask one person to pray, and they would ask their church to pray. These people passed the news to their friends, and the prayers increased, until tens of thousands of people were praying for us. I was humbled, and grateful for the people who blessed us. Dan and I called this "God's social network."

This past week, unexpected help poured in. Each time it did, it was a reminder that God would take care of me, no matter what. Family, friends, and even people I didn't know stepped in and said, "You need help with the boys. We're coming over," or, "We're bringing you dinner tonight." Each act of kindness helped me get through one more hour of the darkness that surrounded me and reminded me that God was still with me.

I thought about all of the miracles Dan and I had experienced over the last week. While it might be assumed that the greatest miracle for us was Dan's safe return to our family, I realized it was not. The greatest miracle was that God, infinitely powerful and holy, was with each of us. Even while he was caring for Dan and me, he was also with the rescuers, with others who were trapped, and with the millions of Haitians impacted by this tragedy. He was with the families and friends of those missing and those who were grieving and waiting for answers. And he was in heaven welcoming the thousands of souls who were receiving their reward in their eternal home.

God didn't turn away when I yelled at him; he didn't abandon me when I wasn't ready to trust him. He accepted me as I am. He walked with me and suffered with me. Not only during my years of depression, but during the past week when I thought my husband was dead. He experienced this pain with me.

It is hard to trust and follow Jesus when we don't know where he is leading or what the result may be. My heart does not always trust the way it should, and my mind often takes me places I shouldn't go.

But now more than ever, I know that all I can do is to follow where he leads.

God delivered me from that deep dark hole of depression. While I know I will always be susceptible to relapses, I also realize that God will help me through them as they come. I'd been through six terrible years of depression at the beginning of our marriage, but we've had ten good years since that rocky start. I have a life with Dan and the boys that I never thought I would have.

I looked down at Dan's hand wrapped around mine. The earthquake had shaken a few things in our marriage that needed to be shaken loose: pettiness, frustration, anger, and impatience. The walls we had built to protect ourselves from getting hurt had become a six-story pile of rubble inside our marriage, and I looked forward to leaving them behind us.

I would never want anything like this devastating earthquake to happen again. Even so, I could already see how God was using it in our marriage. And, more importantly, now I had a greater understanding of how God loves and cares for me — for all of us — during every circumstance of our lives.

I squeezed Dan's hand as the plane picked up speed and then ascended into the bright sky. I felt loved. Loved by Dan and loved by God.

Somehow God had taken this horror-filled experience in our lives and transformed it into something good — something very good.

31

SAVED

Dan

When I got back to Colorado Springs, I had lots of opportunities to share my story on broadcasts like *The Today Show*, *NBC Nightly News*, *Inside Edition*, and *Larry King Live*. Almost every interview I did made some reference to the idea that I was saved by an iPhone app.

I wasn't saved by an iPhone app any more than I was saved by my own efforts. It was very helpful to have a resource to consult while I was treating my wounds, but there were other things as, or even more, influential in my survival — like the survival tips of Bear Grylls that I had learned from, the rescuers who risked their lives to save me, or my strong determination to get home to my wife and boys.

The truth is, *God saved my life*, but that's much harder to talk about. Some people don't want to know much about my faith. They're afraid someone will be offended, or perhaps they just don't believe that there is a God and that he takes care of his children.

The truth is, it's hard for me to say that sometimes too. When I say that God saved me, it opens up so many other questions, the biggest ones being — *Why didn't he save David? Why did so many others die?*

I don't know. I ask myself that question a lot. And I have gotten to the point where I am OK with not knowing the answer. I understand more clearly now that there are things in this life that are beyond my feeble brain's ability to comprehend, and that I can entrust these inscrutable issues to God's loving care.

We do not know when an earthquake may come into our lives or what form it will take. But when it comes, God is not taken by surprise; nor are his plans for us frustrated. In fact, whether God creates the crisis or merely allows it in our lives (a topic beyond the limits of this book), he uses it for his purpose. Earthquakes in our lives shake us — but they can also be used by God to bring about the development of our character and spirit, to fulfill his plans for us. And that's what happened to me. God used the Haiti earthquake to teach Christy and me lessons about trusting him.

Christy has always been uncomfortable with me risking the inherent dangers of travel in poverty-ridden countries. While I loved the rare adventure of overseas travel before this trip to Haiti, I also considered it somewhat risky. I worried what she would be faced with if something happened to me. In other words, we both worried about the exact scenario that happened in Haiti. Over the years, our fears impacted decisions about ministry and career opportunities. We often took what we perceived as the safest choice.

After this latest adventure, Christy and I have a different perspective on risk and safety. It is abundantly clear to us that God intervened to bring me back safely through miracles that are hard to ignore. If God went to these lengths to return me to my unfinished life, I was never truly in an "unsafe" situation. It wasn't my time to die; therefore God kept me alive. Likewise, had it been God's will for my life to end on January 12, staying home wouldn't have prevented it.

In Corrie ten Boom's famous book *The Hiding Place*, her sister Betsie points out to Corrie that the only thing to really focus on is aligning ourselves with God's purposes: "There are no 'ifs' in God's world. And no places that are safer than other places. The center of His will is our only safety."

The illusion of "safe" keeps people unprepared to handle a tragic interruption and keeps them insulated from any sense of urgency to live lives that make a difference in the world. The illusion of "unsafe" keeps people on the sidelines, held back by their fears from the impact they could be having.

So now, as Christy and I evaluate opportunities and their associated risks, we do it differently. Instead of looking only at the risks and asking if we'll be safe, we evaluate these opportunities in the context of God's sovereign plan for our lives. We know that God may call us to risk and sacrifice for his work in the world, and that we can be OK with that — fully assured that he can be trusted, no matter the outcome. We don't use this as a license for recklessness, but instead as an opportunity to demonstrate and live out our renewed trust in God.

There is something about staring at death in the darkness that illuminates our lives. During my sixty-five hours facing death, God shone a light on the way I had recently been living. Under his illumination, I discovered that I had settled for a kind of half life — going through the motions — in some of the most important areas of my life.

I was a follower of Christ, but my relationship with him had become so halfhearted and lukewarm that it could be considered almost insulting to the Creator of the universe and his Son who died on the cross for my sins. It's as if I had been hedging my bets, investing some of my efforts in my own approach to life just in case God's approach didn't work out.

Through my underground encounters with God, I was reminded that the relationship he calls me to is a wholehearted, all-or-nothing commitment, not one foot on God's path and one foot headed in my own direction. I was created to serve and glorify him, and since returning from Haiti, I recommit myself daily to this purpose.

The partial, half-effort approach to my faith had also come to characterize my marriage. Though I have been my wife's partner for our entire seventeen years of marriage, and though I have always strived to show her love, I had allowed many things in our relationship to slip in recent years. We were both aware of the chill that had crept into our marriage, but we didn't know what to do about it, or maybe we weren't motivated enough to figure it out.

Within the first minutes after the quake, I found my motivation as I mourned the possibility I might die with Christy unaware of the extent of my love. Though I tried to remedy this through journal entries that she would find after my death, I also knew that words on a page weren't capable of expressing the fullness of my feelings, or of convincing her that I was still in love with her. I vowed that if I survived, I would fix this problem.

Christy and I had let the busyness of life get in the way of making sure that our relationship was where we wanted it to be, every day. Since my rescue, we've made changes to make sure that we're connecting deeply and not letting our tiredness at the end of a day lead into just watching TV together and saying, "OK, we've connected."

Instead we are intentional about some new practices that have made a significant difference. Every day, without exception, we make sure to spend time — at least a few minutes, sometimes more — in focused, face-to-face conversation. We talk about the things on our minds and our hearts. We allow no interruptions, and whenever possible we try to do this while really looking each other in the eyes. To some this may sound simplistic, but we had come to a place in our marriage where we could go many days, even weeks, without this foundational and intimate kind of connection.

At the end of these conversations, I now ask Christy, "Have we connected the way we need to today? Is there anything else on your heart we need to talk about?" As awkward or stilted as those questions may sound, this one addition to our lives has made a significant difference and paves the way for a richer companionship.

Added to this practice, we now have regular date nights (without kids!) and more times of prayer together. And when we have issues or fights that crop up between us, we have reinstated the practice to never let the night go by without resolving those issues.

With God's grace, I am no longer living a half life; instead, I am living a new kind of life, a life closer to the life Jesus talked about when he said, "I have come that they may have life, and have it to the full." For me, that means living each moment as a precious gift, with an intentional focus on nurturing our marriage and living out my faith.

While I was in Haiti, lots of things were shaken by the earthquake, including how I viewed myself, my marriage, and my faith. But the quake also shook loose a lot of things that weren't important, leaving the solid foundation on which my life is built: my faith and my family. It's ironic to think that I went to Haiti to participate in Compassion's programs that rescue children — *and I ended up being the one who needed rescue.* The Haiti earthquake wasn't the first quake I'd faced, and it won't be the last. However, my experience showed me that whatever is thrown at me doesn't matter.

I can hang on until the shaking stops *because my God is unshakable.*

EPILOGUE

The January 12, 2010, 7.0 magnitude earthquake struck just west of Port-au-Prince, Haiti, and devastated the city and its surrounding communities, crippling the government of Haiti. It is estimated that 230,000 people died, more than 188,000 homes were completely destroyed, and over five million people were directly affected through injuries and loss of family, homes, and jobs, as well as other devastating effects of the natural disaster. Any suffering that I experienced was so minor compared to that of others caught in this tragedy. Please continue to pray for the people of Haiti, especially the children and the poor.

Briefly, here are the stories of some of the people I encountered while I was in Haiti.

Ephraim and Johnnie

My Haitian Compassion guide, Ephraim, was not hurt in the earthquake. After I returned home, I received an e-mail from him telling me his story. His car was about ten feet from the front of the lobby when the hotel collapsed. At first, he didn't know it was an earthquake and didn't understand what had caused the collapse. There was so much dust covering the windows that he couldn't even get out of the car for several minutes. His car was damaged by falling debris that blocked access to the street leading away from the Montana.

Ephraim waited an hour to see if he could find any sign of David or me, but he only saw one man with a broken leg emerge from a very small hole in the rubble. As the sky darkened, Ephraim walked down the hill to the main road. Only when he saw the chaos at the bottom of the hill did he realize there had been an earthquake, and he immediately went to find his family.

Though some of Ephraim's extended family and friends were injured or killed, all of his immediate family survived and are doing well. His twenty-three-year-old daughter, Taliana, was in a university building when the quake struck and was one of only twenty students (out of two hundred) who got out alive. His church also survived and was the only building in his neighborhood left standing. After the earthquake, Ephraim sheltered many people in his house and cared for those in need around him. He wrote to me, "I have just watched your interview from the Internet, and I am more than happy to see your face again, my friend. Above all things, we have the guarantee that one day we will be together in the heaven where tragedy and suffering will have no place."

Our translator, Johnnie, also escaped injury, as did his family, but he had friends and neighbors who were killed. Johnnie is very much in demand as a translator, using his language skills to help Compassion and many other relief organizations that are now working in Port-au-Prince.

Missoul and Other Mothers and Children from Compassion's Programs

The church we had visited on Tuesday was approximately thirty miles farther from the epicenter beyond Port-au-Prince, so there was far less damage to structures there. Missoul and her children survived the earthquake, and their house and their church remain intact.

In the days and months following the quake, Compassion staff and church partners searched diligently through neighborhoods, tent cities, and countryside shelters to account for each of the 65,000 babies, mothers, and children in Compassion's programs in Haiti.

By June, they had accounted for 93 percent of their beneficiaries, and they continue to search for the remaining 1,660 whose status is unknown. Compassion has reported the deaths of 58 babies and children in their programs, with 954 injuries. Many Compassion children also lost parents or siblings. Due to the tremendous outpouring of support from Compassion sponsors, Compassion's network of partner churches was able to provide critical aid to tens of thousands of families — food kits, medical care, emergency shelters — and work on strategies to support long-term recovery.

Jim and the Others Trapped with Him

Jim Gulley, Ann Varghese, Rick Santos, and Sarla Chand all made it out alive and home to the United States safely. They have returned to the humanitarian work they were doing before the earthquake.

Jim has made several trips back to Haiti and has done some speaking about his experiences. We continue to stay in touch via phone and e-mail, and we were reunited at a church in Colorado Springs where we were both invited to speak.

Sadly, the two men trapped with Jim whose legs were pinned didn't survive their injuries. Rev. Clinton Rabb had both legs amputated before he was rescued from the Hotel Montana. On January 17, he died in a Miami hospital. Rev. Sam Dixon died while the rescuers were trying to get him out.

Lukeson

A few weeks after I returned home, I made contact with Lukeson via e-mail. We continue to stay in touch through e-mail and online chats. Lukeson tells me he is doing well. Neither his fiancée nor his mother was hurt in the earthquake. He found a church to attend and reads his Creole Bible every day. He recently told me, "Jesus is everything to me." He still plans to marry his fiancée, though no date has been set. With the Hotel Montana gone, Lukeson continues to look for work in Port-au-Prince.

The Rescuers

I was never able to make sense of what happened with the French rescue team after they freed Jim, Sarla, and the others. My best guess is that the list with our names on it did not get passed on to the next group of rescuers. Another explanation may be that since the rescuers were still working to free Sam Dixon and Clinton Rabb, there may have been confusion among the rescue teams. When someone said, "There are two more left," other rescuers may have thought they were referring to Sam and Clint instead of Lukeson and me.

I am not clear as to whether or not there was a Capitaine. Recent conversations I've had suggest that it may have been Ann, who was interpreting for the French team, and I misunderstood her to be a French rescuer. My mind was pretty confused in those final hours before my rescue.

The American captain who had called out, "I have two new contacts. I need a new crew," was a team captain from Fairfax, Virginia. He initiated the efforts that led to my rescue through the elevator shaft. After encountering difficulty reaching me from where Jim had been trapped, his team looked for other ways to access me, which led to Sam Gray's discovery of the elevator.

Sam returned home to his wife and two girls on January 28. He and his team spent about two and a half weeks in Haiti and helped in many rescues, including saving lives at an orphanage and a university.

On June 15, 2010, Christy and I had the wonderful opportunity to spend an evening with the brave men of the Fairfax, Virginia, search and rescue team, exchanging stories and embracing our new lifelong friends.

David

While in Miami, I passed on pictures and any identifying information I could think of to facilitate David's rescue in case he was still alive. It was nearly a month before his body was found and identified. It was determined that he had indeed died within the first few seconds of the Hotel Montana's collapse.

I continue to be inspired by David's example of how he lived his life: his ministry, his relationships, and his devotion to God. We continue to pray for his family.

The video footage that David captured on our trip was never recovered.

The Woolley Family

Christy and I experienced the love of the body of Christ in new ways through this experience. Dustin, my supervisor at Compassion, and Brent, a pastor from our church, flew to Miami to provide us with love and support while I was in the hospital. We returned to Colorado to find Compassion International staff, family, and friends from church waiting to celebrate our return at the airport.

My reunion with Josh and Nathan the following morning was a life highlight I'll always remember. The boys wanted to start rough-housing right away, but I had to wait a few weeks before my wounds healed enough that I could get back to our usual activities.

My body has healed almost completely, but I will always have the battle scars on my leg and the back of my head. They serve as tangible reminders of the lessons I've learned, and I am grateful for both. I occasionally have nightmares, but for the most part I feel like I have adjusted emotionally as well as I have physically.

I am still at Compassion, creating websites and using social media to spread news about Compassion's work on behalf of "the least of these." My experiences in Haiti have given me opportunities to share my story through speaking, writing, and other media engagements. Learn more at www.DanWoolley.net.

Christy was also forever changed by this experience, and she is discovering new lessons each day as she continues her healing from this crisis. Our lives will never return to the "normal" we had before January 12, nor would she want it to.

She has started a new semester of homeschooling with our boys and continues to run our home business, www.MyKidsWeek.com.

We currently have two trips to Haiti planned, and our hearts will always have a meaningful connection with the people of Haiti — one that we hope to nurture over time.

The boys are doing well. They understand some of what happened to me in Haiti, but not all. Nathan continues to tell people that "Jesus stopped the rocks from hitting Daddy, and Mommy went to Haiti to rescue him."

Though the Haitian earthquake shook our lives in unexpected ways, I readily tell people that the trauma I experienced in Haiti was second to the trauma Christy faced in the six long years she worked to overcome depression. Approximately one in ten adults will suffer from a severe depression in a given year. If you or someone you know is experiencing symptoms of depression, please seek professional help. Rescue from your darkness is possible too.

Finally, I encourage you to support Compassion International. They had been actively working in Haiti for decades before the earthquake, and their work there and in impoverished communities around the world has never been more important. Learn more about Compassion's work in Haiti and around the world, and how you can make a difference in the lives of mothers, babies, and children trapped in poverty, by visiting www.compassion.com/unshaken.

Dan Woolley
July, 2010

ACKNOWLEDGMENTS

There is a fraternity of men (and women) who choose to risk their lives, day in and day out, in order to bring others to safety. Declaring firefighters and search and rescue professionals "heroes" may not be an original sentiment, but I now have such great personal appreciation for the selfless and risky work they do that my understanding of the words *hero* and *bravery* will forever be redefined. So I must begin by thanking the brave men and women of Virginia Task Force 1, the International Urban Search and Rescue team from Fairfax, Virginia, for putting their lives on the line for me and others in Haiti in January, and for doing so in other crises around the world.

I feel especially indebted to my rescuer, Sam Gray, who, after finding a crack in the rubble, said, "I can fit through that hole" and then climbed down through the elevator shaft to the bottom of a collapsed and unstable hotel to be with me and pull me out, embracing the danger for my sake. Because of Sam Gray, William Moreland, Mike Davis, Carlos Carrillo, George Hahn, Evan Lewis, Brian Gillingham, Buck Best, Eddie Thurston, Daryl Casey, Doc MacIntyre, and Teresa MacPherson, I am here to tell my story today. My wife and I can confess no less than love for them, in response to the love they showed me, in the spirit of Jesus' words in John 15:13: "Greater love has no one than this, that he lay down his life for his friends." May God bless all of you and your families, and may you know his peace in your lives.

It has become almost cliché to thank one's wife in the acknowledgments (a smart thing to do for any husband-author!), but my thanks in this case are to my key collaborator, not just my spouse and supporter. I cannot overstate the contribution my wife, Christy, has made to this book. From telling her side of our Haiti experience in the later chapters — some of the most gripping parts of the story — to significant hours spent in editing and rewriting content throughout, this book simply could not have been written without her help. More than anything, though, her willingness to allow me to tell the story of her struggle with depression, and the difficult work she put in to help craft those chapters, showed a rare courage that increases my respect and gratefulness for her all the more. Thank you, Sweet.

Several great salt-of-the-earth people were a part of my story. Thank you for letting me tell your story as part of mine, and please forgive any errors of memory of our shared experiences. Ephraim, Johnnie, and the entire staff at Compassion's Haiti office, thank you for everything you do every day for "the least of these" and for hosting me so well on my short visit. Lukeson, thanks for being my companion under the Montana and my friend since our rescue. Rick Santos, Ann Varghese, and Jim Gulley, thank you for the camaraderie and encouragement you provided while we shared our challenging adventure. And Sarla, you will always be a hero to me for your bravery in reaching out to rescuers, which I did my best to describe from the perspective of one listening in the dark.

I recognize that while my story ended well for me and my family, many others — some American families and millions of Haitian families — suffered profound losses. For all who lost loved ones in this tragedy, you have my sincere and heartfelt sympathy.

While I was facing my challenges in Haiti, Christy was enduring her own trial in Colorado Springs, and I am grateful for all who came to her aid, offering love, prayers, and, where possible, logistical and material support. Special thanks to Marti and Jim Schroeder, Anna, Valerie, Cara, my sisters Renee Cortez and Miriam Frost, Tonya Menuey, Dave and Holly Rhody, Ken and Meredith Norwood, Michael and Wendy Fox, Bryant and Lauren Swenson, Gloria Thuon, Melanie Reynolds, Monique Saade, Kevin Wheeler, Diane and Kevin Rohan, Connie Cram, Suzie Martin, Deb Brown, Monica Staab, Gillian Rosenthal, Leslie Mullin, and friends from David C. Cook, Azusa Pacific University, Russ Reid, and African Enterprise. I'm sure many others should be mentioned here as well. Please forgive any omissions, and thank you all for taking such good care of my wife and boys when I couldn't.

Thanks to Jean and Donald Pullen, Lois and Herb Rader, John and Peg Merwin, Janet and Mark Hall, and Judy and Jim Kerns for mobilizing prayer for our family and sustaining Jim and Marti with love and emotional support while they aided us.

I am indebted to Caitlin, Elizabeth, and Matthew Fuentes, to administrators Bob Clark and Angela Bridges, and to hundreds of contributors who made the Haiti Earthquake Hotel Montana Facebook page a lifeline of information and support for family and friends of those missing in the quake, including my loved ones while I was lost. Thanks for creating a community where thousands of strangers became family — truly showing the best of humanity coming together in a crisis.

I feel a deep sense of gratitude and love for my Compassion International family, in Colorado Springs and around the world, who prayed for me when I was lost and celebrated with me when I returned. Those celebrations were like a taste of heaven for me. Rick Davis, I will always be in awe of your efforts to secure my rescue and your care for my family during impossible circumstances. Thanks to others at Compassion who lovingly supported my family or assisted in efforts to find me, especially Victoria Stoner, Wess Stafford, Rich Van Pelt, Bob Thorp, Mike Johnson, Dustin Hardage, Natalie Gbandawa, Kathy Redmond, Brad Barker, Scott Barnes, Edouard Lassegue, and Guilbaud Saint-Cyr. I'm sure dozens more sprang into action in ways I am not even aware of, and many of you have encouraged me and helped me adjust to new realities since my return — especially my pho friends and the web team. Thank you, friends.

Thanks to Chuck Cichowitz from Noah's Ark Whitewater Rafting Co., Rob Williams, and Rich Van Pelt, who were ready to drop everything and mobilize their own rescue team to bring me back.

Many people have told me how they agonized in prayer for me and my family as they asked God for a miraculous rescue. Family, friends, past acquaintances, and even complete strangers around the world put their lives on hold for several days, many giving up sleep to cry out to God on our behalf. Seeing such an overflow of God's love in others humbles me and inspires me to invest more of my life in intercession for others. To those who prayed for us during this trial, I offer my sincerest thanks. Though prayer remains a mystery to me, I do know that God heard each of these prayers and that they played a part in the miracles of my survival and rescue.

Thanks to my agent, Kathy Helmers, and the entire team at Creative Trust, who believed in me and my story enough to take it to publishers and encouraged me along the way in this new world of authorship that I knew so little about. Thank you to my friends at Zondervan: my editors, Sandy Vander Zicht and Dirk Buursma, for your patient guidance and stewardship of the content, kindly administered; to interior design experts Sarah Johnson and Beth Shagene, for your creative handling of the presentation of the text on each page and your masterful work on the photo insert section; to Don Gates and Robin Geelhoed, for your consistent show of support for this story and for your creative marketing ideas; and to others at Zondervan, who teamed together to take this story to the world. Thanks to Amy Anderson and others at the DeMoss Group for shepherding us through experiences with the media.

I'm especially grateful to my cowriter Jennifer Schuchmann, not only for so quickly helping me turn my story into a book worth reading, but for the way you demonstrated patience and a diligent work ethic throughout, all the while encouraging my own writing skills and interests.

Thanks to my manuscript readers, Nydia Teter, Scott Barnes, Joe Cunningham, Bryant Swensen, Beth, Paul Moede, John McKeever, Marti Schroeder, Anna Austin, Valerie Skaret, and Sam Bhat, for your encouragement and essential feedback that helped me refine the story line and messages of the book. Special thanks to Susan Tjaden, who stepped in at key times with editorial heroics.

I feel especially indebted to a few friends who showed faith in me and this story through words of encouragement at significant moments: Wess Stafford, Matt Heard, Jimmy Dodd, Rich Van Pelt, Jon Wallace, Don Pape, Phyllis Wallace, Chris Fabry, Mark Nelessen, Mark Tatum, Beth, Chad Arnold, Coco Muse, Tonya Menuey, Tammy Horvath, and Karl Schaller. Without these conversations, the ministry of this story and book would not have happened.

Thanks to Bear Grylls for your shows that inspired me to do whatever it took to stay alive. Thanks to Randy Wilson, author of *Celebrations of Faith*, from whom we discovered the idea of the Joshua Basket (which we called "Jordan Basket"). Thanks to Francis Chan, whose book *Crazy Love* was already challenging me to a new level of sold-out devotion to God before my trip to Haiti. Thanks to Ken Gire, Randy Alcorn, John Piper, Anne Graham Lotz, and Philip Yancey, who serve as wise counselors as I work to understand God's love and sovereignty in the midst of suffering. Those interested in these topics can find an annotated list of resources at www .DanWoolley.net.

At a point of great distress early Wednesday morning, I decided to expend an hour of my iPhone battery to listen to some music in the dark. The playlist I listened to (now nicknamed "Songs from a Broken Elevator") was perfectly formed to lift my spirits. Thanks to Phillips, Craig & Dean; Jeremy Camp; MercyMe; Aaron Shust; Tim Hughes; Switchfoot; Michael W. Smith; Newsboys; Stuart Townend; Natalie Grant; Nichole Nordeman; Chris Rice; Nicole C. Mullen; Casting Crowns; and Chris Tomlin for ministering to my heart and helping to usher me into God's presence when I needed encouragement.

And to Mark Bornstein, thanks for authoring your version of Psalm 40 that helped to "lift me out of the pit and set my feet on a rock."

I would be remiss not to thank several people who conspired to make me who I am today. Thanks to my mom, who has stood with me through many trials and who taught me how to pray in faith to the God of miracles, resurrection power, and fatherly love. Thanks to my sisters — Karen, Donna, Mimmy, and Renee — who shaped so much of my character and personality and who love me better than I deserve. And to Jim and Marti, whose involvement in my life makes me a better person. You are all dear to my heart.

———

Christy also wanted to thank some people personally for their help and support:

Thank you, Claudia, for being my personal angel in Miami. Dustin and Brent, thanks for being family for us so that we were not alone in the hospital. You each set aside everything to take care of us. God knew the three of you were just what we needed.

Valerie and Brian, Anna and Benjamin, and Cara: Thank you for loving us, praying for us, taking care of Josh and Nathan, and supporting us in every way you could. I love you all so much.

Tonya, Meredith, and Holly: Thank you for helping with so many details during this crisis, offering your listening ears and caring for me so tenderly. You are dear to me.

Our friends at Woodmen Valley Chapel: Thank you for being the body of Christ in tangible ways for us, for prayers and for stepping in when you saw a need. Thanks to my Awana colleagues for being my sweet friends. Thanks to Erin Locket for being my night shift support.

Mom and Dad: You both have sacrificed so much, putting your lives aside and exhausting yourself physically and emotionally to help us through this challenging time. Thank you for your love in our lives.

Beth: Thank you, my dear friend, for saving my life and teaching me new ways to live.

Dear Reader,

I love these photos because they remind me of why I went to Haiti in the first place.

Witness the love in Missoul's eyes. It broke my heart to realize that although moms like Missoul love their babies every bit as much as Christy and I love our boys, extreme poverty robs children like Micheleine from the potential they could have in life. In fact, too many babies in Haiti do not even reach their fifth birthday—victims of preventable diseases or malnutrition. And many are sold as restaveks (child slaves) under the false hope for a better life.

But we are in a position to change that—to stop poverty before it stamps its mark permanently on a child's life. Compassion's Child Survival Program in Haiti is changing the reality for thousands of mothers and their babies, providing:

- nutritious food and supplements
- vaccinations and ongoing health care
- parenting education and encouragement
- spiritual nurturing and a faith community
- income-generating opportunities

Your support can literally mean the difference between life and death for a young vulnerable child. I have held babies who are alive today because of this program, and I've met mothers who have real hope for their children's future for the first time because of the help and guidance they are receiving. And after this devastating earthquake, the needs are more urgent than ever.

Life is short, and we don't know when our time on this earth will be over. So it's imperative that we live our lives in ways that make a difference now and for eternity. If you are moved by the needs of children in poverty, please do something about it. Today. Right now.

To learn about Compassion's Child Survival Program and discover how you can change the trajectory of a child's life, please visit Compassion.com/unshaken.

May you grow in a faith that stands unshaken,

Dan Woolley

Share Your Thoughts

With the Author: Your comments will be forwarded to the author when you send them to *zauthor@zondervan.com*.

With Zondervan: Submit your review of this book by writing to *zreview@zondervan.com*.

Free Online Resources at
www.zondervan.com

Zondervan AuthorTracker: Be notified whenever your favorite authors publish new books, go on tour, or post an update about what's happening in their lives at www.zondervan.com/authortracker.

Daily Bible Verses and Devotions: Enrich your life with daily Bible verses or devotions that help you start every morning focused on God. Visit www.zondervan.com/newsletters.

Free Email Publications: Sign up for newsletters on Christian living, academic resources, church ministry, fiction, children's resources, and more. Visit www.zondervan.com/newsletters.

Zondervan Bible Search: Find and compare Bible passages in a variety of translations at www.zondervanbiblesearch.com.

Other Benefits: Register yourself to receive online benefits like coupons and special offers, or to participate in research.

ZONDERVAN®

ZONDERVAN.com/
AUTHORTRACKER
follow your favorite authors